Building Ideas

Building Ideas

An Introduction to Architectural Theory

Jonathan A Hale

JOHN WILEY & SONS, LTD
Chichester • New York • Weinheim • Brisbane • Singapore • Toronto

Copyright © 2000 by John Wiley & Sons Ltd,
Baffins Lane, Chichester,
West Sussex PO19 1UD, England

National   01243 779777
International   (+44) 1243 779777

e-mail (for orders and customer service enquiries): cs-books@wiley.co.uk
Visit our Home Page on   http://www.wiley.co.uk
          or   http://www.wiley.com

Library of Congress Cataloging-in-Publication Data
Hale, Jonathan.
   Building ideas: an introduction to architectural theory/Jonathan Hale.
      p. cm.
   Includes bibliographical references and index.
   ISBN 0-471-85194-9 (alk. paper)
   1. Architecture—Philosophy. I. Title.

NA2500 .H235 2000
720'.1—dc21
                                                    99-052985

British Library Cataloguing in Publication Data
A catalogue record for this book is available from the British Library

ISBN 0-471-85194-9

Typeset in 10/12pt Times by Wyvern 21 Ltd, Bristol
Printed and bound in Great Britain by Bookcraft (Bath) Ltd

This book is printed on acid-free paper responsibly manufactured from sus-
tainable forestry, in which at least two trees are planted for each one used
for paper production.

Contents

Acknowledgements

This book grew out of a seminar course I was lucky enough to teach at Drexel University, Philadelphia, in the summer of 1996. I must initially thank Paul Hirshorn for the opportunity to try out some of this material, as well as a lively group of students for their input and interest in the course. The research for the book began at the University of Pennsylvania, under the somewhat formidable guidance of Joseph Rykwert, Marco Frascari and David Leatherbarrow who together managed to open up a rich historical background to many of the debates in contemporary architecture. I am also indebted to the Thouron family for their generous financial support, which allowed me the opportunity to undertake postgraduate study.

I must also thank my undergraduate teachers for their inspiration and encouragement, particularly Patrick Hodgkinson, Michael Brawne and Peter Smithson, without whom even thinking about architecture might never have occurred to me. Ted Cullinan deserves a special mention for providing me with the experience of enjoying the way buildings are put together, as well as the opportunity to combine practice with teaching in a stimulating and supportive environment.

I would also like to record a vote of thanks to all those who have influenced my thinking in various ways over the years, as well as those who have made a specific contribution to the making of this book, including Tim Anstey, Stephanie Baker, Mark Beedle, Tom Coward, David Dernie, Mary Ann Duffy, Terrance Galvin, Bill Hutson, Neil Leach, Christine Macy, Donald Wilson and, in particular, all my colleagues at the University of Nottingham.

I am indebted to Maggie Toy and everyone at Wiley's for their confidence in the idea behind this book. Lastly, I must thank my parents and also my wife, Jocelyn Dodd, for being there and for still being there.

Note on the Bibliography

To assist in the use of this book as a set text for architectural theory courses, a list of suggestions for further reading has been provided relevant to themes covered in each chapter. The first two sections in each list – described as "background" and "foreground" – relate to the approximate division within each chapter between the philosophical and the architectural material. Both sections typically refer to readily accessible sources, either for reference or further reading on a topic of particular interest. The third section includes suggestions for possible seminar readings, which have been chosen to highlight key issues in the debates surrounding each topic. These are also selected from readily available sources, usually from anthologies of architectural theory or commonly accessible journals.

Introduction

Theoretical Practices

In a chapter called "Demonstrations" in his book *Monsters of Architecture*, the architectural theorist Marco Frascari describes the relation of drawing to building as follows:

> The traditional interpretation of this translation is that an architectural drawing is a graphic representation of an existing, or future building. The present modern and post-modern condition of understanding . . . these translations is that buildings are *representations of the drawings that preceded them.*[1]

A glance at the recent history of significant events in architecture would confirm the importance of "things-other-than-buildings" in the dissemination of architectural ideas. The Victorian rediscovery of Greek polychrome decoration – upsetting centuries of scholarship based on the assumption of a "white" architecture – is one such event of historical importance which emerged from documentary sources, rather than the fabric of the buildings themselves. More recently this phenomenon has taken several surprising twists, not least due to the growing impact of photographic representation. One of the most iconic and characteristic of twentieth century buildings is the Barcelona Pavilion designed by Ludwig Mies van der Rohe. Built in 1929 for the International Exposition, the Pavilion was demolished in the following

---

[1] Marco Frascari, *Monsters of Architecture: Anthropomorphism in Architectural Theory*, Rowman and Littlefield, Savage, MD, 1991, p 93 [emphasis added].

year along with the other temporary structures. From a set of black and white photographs – some carefully retouched for effect – the building became known across the world through publications on modern architecture. Nearly all subsequent commentary on this "touchstone" of modernity was made by those who had never seen the building, except in these much reproduced photographs.

A similar process has taken place in the spread of foreign influences in America, such as Frank Lloyd Wright's famous inspiration by the architecture of Japan, after seeing the Ho-O-Den pavilion in Chicago at the 1893 World's Fair. From the 1932 MOMA show called "The International Style" to the same museum's 1988 exhibition on "Deconstructivist Architecture" – both of which have had a huge impact on the production of architecture in North America – the influence of other media on the transmission of architectural ideas can often far outweigh that of the experience of the buildings themselves. Whether in books, films or exhibitions, or as part of a general cultural debate, architectural concepts exist on a plane distinct from their embodiment in particular buildings. This is not to say that the two realms can ever be separated from each other, merely that "built objects" form just one component within a larger network of "architectural phenomena."

Daniel Libeskind's design for the Jewish Museum in Berlin is a prime example of the reputation of a building preceding its construction by several years. So many publications have presented this project at various stages during its completion that, like the Barcelona Pavilion, it has taken on a life of its own through drawings and photographs. This situation can lead to a disenchantment with the apparent transience of our "media society", such as implied by Jean Baudrillard's book entitled *The Gulf War Did Not Take Place*, where he suggested that the "news event" had become more important than reality. A more positive understanding of this new fluency of ideas would accept that the media event is also a valid component of reality. Likewise, in architecture this idea is an important factor in our understanding, which is always the result of a "collision" between imagination and experience.

The publication of polemical projects has also increased rapidly in recent years, in journals such as *Architectural Design* as well as the many school-based periodicals. Peter Eisenman and Jacques Derrida's collaboration entitled *Chora L Works*, and Libeskind's facsimile set of working documents from the V & A project, show how these presentations have added to an earlier "currency", in which new ideas have circulated in the form of "manifestoes" and theoretical statements. The recent appearance of a whole series of anthologies containing reprints of theoretical writings has also served to increase awareness of the wider influences affecting architecture. The crossover between debates going on in other areas of cultural inquiry has begun to shift architectural thinking towards the field of "cultural theory". The persistent presence of architectural issues in a whole range of theoretical debates – in fields such as anthropology, psycho-geography, film and media studies – has even led to an interest in the occurrence of architectural ideas within the very structure of philosophy itself.

The architectural theorist Mark Wigley has written at length on this relationship, looking at the reliance on – and simultaneous denial of – the role of architectural metaphors in the history of philosophical thinking. The grand conceptual "edifice" built on "foundations" of truth and certainty has been a common feature in the "construction" of many philosophical systems and likewise, in the present climate of interdisciplinary investigations, there is a marked preoccupation with philosophical thinking in architecture. One of the consequences of this new interest in the broader context of architectural theory is the further blurring of the distinction between "thinking" and "doing". This has led to the notion of a "theoretical practice" that is both critical and constructive in its attitude towards reality. The common characteristic of all these various strategies of practice is the belief in architecture as a mode of cultural discourse. The role of theory in the present climate is a long way from methodology, in that the point is not just about how to make "better" buildings. In terms of the old adage that "society only gets the architecture it deserves", the influence of architectural theory might impact rather upon society, and even help to create the conditions within which a more critical architecture can flourish. The general premise behind all of this reasoning – as well as the motivation for writing this book – is a belief in the significance of architecture as a means of communication, in addition to its ostensible function as a provider of useful space. This distinction sets up the demand for a "hermeneutics" of architecture which would outline the various strategies that might be employed in its interpretation. As should become clear from the opposition set out in Part 1 of this book, even this notion has been the subject of much argument in recent years.

The overall structure of this book reflects the characteristics of our times, in which a plurality of "world views" has come to replace a single outlook. In another age (that perhaps never actually existed), critical strategies might have been ordered according to a dominant "master narrative". Whether theological, philosophical or – since the enlightenment – scientific, this idea of a prevailing doctrine has been weakened in recent years. As philosophers of science have even begun to question its all-encompassing claim to truth, alternative ways of describing the world have again become valid in this new context. The French philosopher Jean-François Lyotard in his book *The Postmodern Condition* claimed its defining characteristic to be the collapse of traditional master-narratives. Through the loss of religious consensus and doubt about the completion of scientific knowledge, Lyotard suggested that communication in society had become fragmented into "language-games". There is nothing frivolous, however, implied by the concept of "games", as it is meant to suggest systems of rules and conventions that might apply to interpretation according to the particular context of the enquiry.

Part 1 addresses this general dilemma over the question of interpretation in architecture, by opposing two definitions based on different attitudes to "meaning". The first considers architecture purely as engineering, with no pretension to communicate, merely to construct useful space. In its idealised form this approach attempts to sidestep the question of meaning, with the input of the designer simply governed by the formula "form follows function". That this can often conceal a deeper agenda – such as the expression of a "machine-aesthetic" – shows how this apparently neutral design process is still subject to cultural forces. The dominant model of scientific rationality in the architectural production of the twentieth century is shown to result from a particular ideology based on the myth of progress in the philosophy of history. Chapter 2 sets out an opposing view, by presenting architecture as a fine art – the emphasis now being on expression rather than functional considerations. This time, in its pure form, the approach tends towards an "autonomous" practice, where the designer takes the role of protagonist in a critical dialogue with the conditions of society. The artist as entertainer, critic, or social conscience are all potential models for the role of theorist or designer using architectural ideas as a means of expression. The philosophical background to this "critical" and expressive approach to architecture is shown to be part of the wider debate concerning the importance of aesthetic experience. Throughout the history of philosophy this theme has resurfaced and has more recently been the site of the great "two cultures" debate – the deterministic laws of science against the free will of the creative artist.

The potential for architecture to act as a critical tool for communication and a means of opening up new experiences of space, is seen as a function of how buildings are perceived and interpreted, and this is the subject of the second part of this book. In this section, three different interpretive strategies are laid out, based on the three main schools of thought within twentieth century philosophy. Each one is shown to impact on the way we think about architecture, and each is illustrated with a range of buildings to show their implications for architectural practice. The themes overlap inasmuch as they can be seen often within the same building, whether part of the design intention or merely possible interpretive strategies. This blurring of "creation" with the process of criticism is part of the agenda of this book, to consider different ways of thinking about buildings, whether as designers or interpreters.

Chapters 3, 4 and 5 consider a range of interpretive models, from the "subjective" to the "objective", depending on their philosophical orientation. Chapter 3, on phenomenology, emphasises the first of these characteristics, by focusing on the perceptual experience of the individual person or subject. The difficulty of generalising from this basically subjective experience, in order to reach a level of shared understanding and communication, is addressed in different ways in Chapters 4 and 5, which look at other more objective factors that might structure our experience. Both of these look at forces – beyond the individual's control – that affect how we perceive things and ultimately, how we communicate. Structuralism, in Chapter 4, considers the deep structures of language and Chapter 5 looks at Marxism, the "invisible" influence of ideology. All three themes offer possibilities as conceptual frameworks for understanding architecture and the conclusion suggests their integration as part of a broader hermeneutic project.

In order to use this book as an introduction to the exploration of theoretical issues, I have included a list of further reading that should serve to amplify the individual themes. Where possible these have been drawn from the recently published anthologies of theoretical texts, in order that this book should also serve as a kind of "road-map" for further study.

Suggestions For Further Reading

Background

Terry Eagleton, *Literary Theory: An Introduction*, University of Minnesota Press, Minneapolis, 1983.

Richard Kearney, *Modern Movements in European Philosophy*, Manchester University Press, Manchester, 1986.

John Lechte, *Fifty Key Contemporary Thinkers: From Structuralism to Postmodernity*, Routledge, London, 1994.

Foreground

Ulrich Conrads (ed.), *Programmes and Manifestoes on 20th Century Architecture*, Lund Humphries, London, 1970.

Mark Gelernter, *Sources of Architectural Form: A Critical History of Western Design Theory*, Manchester University Press, Manchester, 1995.

K. Michael Hays (ed.), *Architecture Theory Since 1968*, MIT Press, Cambridge, MA, 1998.

Charles Jencks and Karl Kropf (eds), *Theories and Manifestoes of Contemporary Architecture*, Academy Editions, London, 1997.

Neil Leach (ed.), *Rethinking Architecture: A Reader in Cultural Theory*, Routledge, London, 1997.

Kate Nesbitt (ed.), *Theorising a New Agenda for Architecture: An Anthology of Architectural Theory 1965-1995*, Princeton Architectural Press, New York, 1996.

Joan Ockman (ed.), *Architecture Culture 1943-1968: A Documentary Anthology*, Rizzoli, New York, 1993.

Readings

K. Michael Hays, "Introduction", in *Architecture Theory Since 1968*, MIT Press, Cambridge, MA, 1998, pp x–xv.

Alberto Perez-Gomez, "Introduction to Architecture and the Crisis of Modern Science", in K. Michael Hays (ed.), *Architecture Theory Since 1968*, MIT Press, Cambridge, MA, 1998, pp 466–75.

Part 1

The Question of Meaning in Architecture

1

Architecture as Engineering
The Technological Revolution

When the new headquarters building for Lloyds of London was completed in 1986 the public reaction was understandably confused. Instead of the traditional image for a city institution of a classical temple standing for permanence and solidity, the insurers – not a profession famed for taking unnecessary risks – had chosen to erect themselves a gigantic piece of pulsating machinery. The associations were clear for all to see: the exposed structure like an oil rig with its spars and platforms, the shiny metal stairs and toilet-pods all piled up like freight containers and clipped on to the outside, and the whole thing capped off with a small army of rooftop cranes – not there just to help build it but there to help *rebuild* it too, when the components wear out and new ones are swung in to take over. Despite the building's improbable appearance, its architect, Sir Richard Rogers, presents his ideas as the most logical response to the demand for flexibility – as he himself has described in a book called *Architecture: A Modern View*:

> If one can access and change short-life parts of a building, its total lifespan can be extended. Lloyds is clearly divided into a long-life central zone housing people and a short-life external zone containing technology.[1]

[1] Richard Rogers, *Architecture: A Modern View*, Thames and Hudson, London, 1990, p 53.

1 Richard Rogers Partnership – Lloyds Building, London, 1978-86. (Alistair Gardner)

Since the Lloyds building was finished, Rogers has gone on to complete a number of substantial projects in a similar idiom, from the spiky steel and glass headquarters of Channel 4 in London (1994) to the more curvaceous forms of the Strasbourg European Court of Human Rights and the Bordeaux Law Courts (1995 and 1998). He is now engaged on a new office building for the German car giants Daimler-Benz, in the centre of Berlin. Rogers' former partner (and fellow recipient of a knighthood for his contribution to British architecture) Norman Foster, has likewise assembled an impressive portfolio of significant international commissions – not least of which, the Hong Kong and Shanghai Bank headquarters – was completed in the same year as Lloyds and embodies a similar range of architectural preoccupations. Since then Foster has completed the Commerzbank in Frankfurt (1997), the Hong Kong International Airport (1998) and most recently the refurbishment of the Reichstag in Berlin, which became the seat of the unified German government on its completion in 1999. In terms of cultural facilities, Foster has also been extremely successful, with additions to the Royal Academy buildings in London (1991), the Carré d'Art in Nimes, France (1993) and the Joslyn Art Museum in Omaha, Nebraska (1994) and he is currently remodelling the courtyard and Reading Room of the British Museum in London.

By any standards, what has become known as the British "high-tech" tradition (though other adherents such as Jean Nouvel in France and Rafael Viñoly in the USA have enjoyed somewhat similar success) is a powerful force in contemporary architecture and deserves a careful and critical analysis – not least because its theoretical underpinnings have a far wider influence on the production of buildings today beyond those that proclaim their origins as explicitly as the examples mentioned above. To begin this analysis it will be necessary to carry out an archaeological "excavation", in order to peel back the accumulated layers of recent practice to uncover its conceptual "ground".

2 Foster and Partners – Renault Distribution Centre, Swindon, 1980–82. (Alistair Gardner)

Twentieth Century Architecture – The Dominance of the Machine

The first layer consists of the building that set the pattern for the current love affair between the world's commercial and civic institutions and the idea of the building as a machine – the Pompidou Centre in Paris, completed in 1977. Designed by Richard Rogers and Renzo Piano together with the engineer Ted Happold, the building responded to the demands of the competition brief for what we now refer to as a "mediatheque", containing art galleries, temporary exhibitions, library, cafés and a research centre for music and acoustics. The competition drawings show not a building so much as a huge steel grid structure hung with escalators and giant cinema-screens facing a plaza – here the functions also seem to have migrated to the space outside, along with the bones and guts of the building. In the competition report the architects describe the structure as a "live centre of information" connected to a network of other centres, such as universities and town halls, across the country. With the plaza as a gathering place and the façade as a display board, the building is conceived as a means of engagement with information, rather than an object of contemplation in its own right. With its moveable floors and vast clear-span spaces, the whole thing was set up as a mechanical instrument for the efficient execution of cultural exchange.

The subsequent popularity of the Pompidou Centre among visitors to the French capital has much to do with its shock value as an architectural novelty, as well as its use as a viewing platform with a vista over the city, rather than its designers' intention of providing a "neutral" container for cultural activities. While in the public perception it still stands out as a spectacular intervention in the otherwise rather staid Parisian street scene, the building has not been so kindly received in the circles of architectural and cultural criticism, as will become clearer later in this discussion. The reasons for its lukewarm reception in some quarters were partly due to the history of the ideas behind it and the fact that as a concept it had been anticipated some years earlier in the work of the British Archigram group, in a series of unbuilt but

3 Piano & Rogers – Pompidou Centre, Paris, 1971–77. (Alistair Gardner)

4 Piano & Rogers – Pompidou Centre, Paris, 1971–77. (Jonathan Hale)

well publicised projects. By the time Rogers' practice, Team 4, (with Su Rogers and Norman and Wendy Foster) was established in the late 1960s the Archigram group had set out what was to become a series of uncannily prescient models for a high-technology, open-ended architecture of infrastructure, to be imitated and also partly realised by a variety of other architects over the subsequent years. Among the most notable were Michael Webb's design for the Furniture Manufacturers Association Headquarters of 1958 with its expressive clustering of circulation and service towers; Cedric Price's Fun Palace of 1961–64 with its throwaway collection of pods and escalators under a membrane roof; and Warren Chalk's Capsule Tower of 1964 with its crane-topped central mast supporting a vast array of anonymous living "containers".

While many of these ideas are paralleled in the preoccupations of the Japanese Metabolist group, who were working on similar possibilities around the same time, the ideological assumptions behind this group of projects are actually quite distinct. For the Japanese, concerned with the acute problems of post-war overcrowding in city centres and the chronic pressures on land use in the country as a whole, the possibilities of minimal living units piled up in tower blocks had a necessary logic behind it. The British work, on the other hand, had a much more playful air to it, premised as it was on issues like the desire for sensory stimulation and the very 1960s preoccupation with the pursuit of pleasure and a libertarian lifestyle. One project that neatly summed up the group's concerns was the "Cushicle" or "Suitaloon" device, again by Michael Webb, which provided a portable enclosure for a single person with sufficient technological apparatus to produce a totally self-contained environment. This highly seductive indulgence in the imagery of the new space age technologies shows a neglect of the need for architecture to support life in the public realm – although the rhetoric of the group rarely addresses such traditional everyday concerns. As the critic Reyner Banham, the great champion of the machine aesthetic, remarked in a 1972 book on the group, Archigram were "short on theory and long on draughtsmanship . . .".[2]

That Banham should raise this paradox of a seemingly rational application of the products of new technology – here being forced into some highly irrational uses – highlights the conflicting forces at work in the theoretical climate of the time. The same writer had raised a similar concern about another of high-tech's obvious antecedents, the British movement from the 1950s known as the New Brutalism. In the subtitle of Banham's 1966 book called *The New Brutalism: Ethic or Aesthetic?* lurks the lingering uncertainty about the real motivations behind the barefaced display of raw concrete, water pipes and electrical conduit boxes that soon became the trademark of what was turning into a style. The mention of "style" in this context set alarm

---

[2] Reyner Banham, quoted in Peter Cook (ed.) *Archigram*, Studio Vista, London, 1972, p 5.

bells ringing in the circles of "rational" modernist architectural criticism, particularly as the stated intentions of the movement's most outspoken advocates, Alison and Peter Smithson, were, revealingly, to be "objective" about reality.

The Smithsons were part of a tight circle of architects and artists based around the Architectural Association and the Institute of Contemporary Arts in London in the 1950s and, through a series of projects both built and unrealised, they also had a major influence on the work of the Archigram group. The brick, steel and glass school at Hunstanton in Norfolk (1949-54), the megastructural composition of the Sheffield University competition of 1953 and the curvaceous fibreglass form of the "House of the Future" of 1956 together contain a range of highly influential ideas. The "brutal" expression of technology and "truth to materials" and the metropolitan-scale infrastructures and systems of movement were to become fundamental principles for much of the architecture which followed, including the work of the Team X (Team 10) group which the Smithsons were also responsible for coordinating. The British architect James Stirling and the American Louis Kahn, who were both invited participants at Team X conferences around 1960, produced two other significant buildings which also had a huge impact on the technology-driven architecture of the subsequent decades. Stirling and Gowan's Leicester University Engineering Building of 1959 and Louis Kahn's Richards Laboratories at the University of Pennsylvania (1957-64) both displayed the dramatic articulation of functional and structural form characteristic of the later Archigram work. In Kahn's case, his project even embodied the "served" and "servant" spaces distinction that later became a key high-tech principle, which was echoed in the Lloyds building's separation of short-life and long-life elements.

In the Smithsons' later writings they appeared to accept the latent paradox inherent in the architect's role as both engineer and artist, in terms of the importance of translating the "tools" that technology provides into a visual and spatial language. With a book entitled *Without Rhetoric: An Architectural Aesthetic* published in 1973, they acknowledged the necessity of the architect's creative input into the process of

5 Stirling and Gowan – Leicester University Engineering Buildings, Leicester, 1959–63. (Neil Jackson)

design, beyond the simple application of technical solutions to the straightforward problems of providing enclosure.

Champion of Technology – Buckminster Fuller

In the 1950s, meanwhile, the air was still heavy with the promise of a coming technological Utopia as the dreams of the pre-war modernists, having been disrupted by the years of conflict, were now being revived by the promise of a period of rapid reconstruction. The mood of optimism in the immediate post-war years was perhaps best summed up by the reaction in the world of architectural theory to the work of the American architect, engineer and inventor, Richard Buckminster

6 Stirling and Gowan – Leicester University Engineering Buildings, Leicester, 1959–63. (Neil Jackson)

7 Louis I Kahn – Richards Medical Research Laboratories, University of
Pennsylvania, 1957–64. (Alistair Gardner)

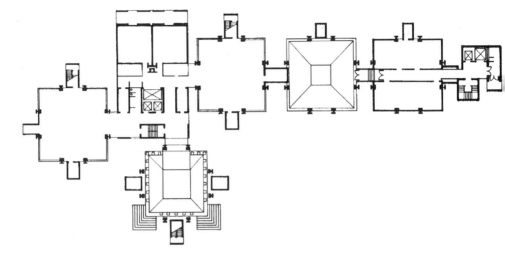

8 Louis I Kahn – Richards Medical Research Buildings, University of Pennsylvania, 1957–64: Entrance level plan. (Redrawn by the author, after Louis I Kahn)

Fuller. Probably the only architect to have an atomic particle named after him ("Buckminsterfullerene", a molecule of carbon which has a similar structure to his "geodesic dome"), Fuller is perhaps best known for the dome he constructed for the 1967 Exposition in Montréal, Canada, based on the geodesic principle and still standing today, though without its original Plexiglass covering. As a tireless innovator of new materials and technologies Fuller had become famous for a series of mass-production prototypes such as the "Dymaxion" series of bathrooms, cars and ultimately houses, from the 1920s to the 1940s, which found only limited practical application but significant theoretical interest. One of Fuller's great apologists in this period of ferment in the 1950s was the English critic Reyner Banham who took up his technological cause and gave it an "academic" respectability. It was largely through Banham's enthusiastic promotion that Fuller's ideas of a technology-driven modern architecture fed into the work of the Archigram group, although Banham was also concerned to establish a sense of historical continuity between these new technological

9 Murphy and Mackey – Geodesic Dome, St. Louis "Climatron", 1960. (Neil Jackson)

innovations and the spirit of the pre-war architecture – now seen as in need of reassessment.

From Banham's point of view the "white architecture" of the 1920s and 1930s had failed to live up to the promise of the great rallying cry of early modernism – Le Corbusier's famous claim from 1923 that a house is a "machine for living in"[3] – and he saw Fuller, finally, as the herald of a true machine-age architecture. In Banham's best-known book called *Theory and Design in the First Machine Age* (1960) he compared Fuller's innovations in the Dymaxion House project from the late 1920s to the allegedly "technically obsolete" architecture of Le Corbusier's Villa Savoye – designed and built around the same time and

---

[3] Le Corbusier, *Towards a New Architecture*, translated by Frederick Etchells, Architectural Press, London, 1946, pp 12–13.

acknowledged by most architectural critics as a classic example of the New Architecture that modernists strove to achieve. The Dymaxion, however, with its circular drum of living space suspended from a central Duralumin mast housing all the mechanical services was, to Banham, the true realisation of Le Corbusier's notion of the "mass-production house". It was, for him, a pioneering example of the kind of pure "technology transfer" as well as the "served and servant spaces" arrangement that were to become basic principles of the developing high-tech tradition. Like the later geodesic dome projects which simplified the form of the Dymaxion house into a skeletal sheltering roof structure made of repeated modular components, Fuller's ideas were presented as the inevitable outcome of the efficient use of the latest new materials. He disparaged the seemingly trivial preoccupations of architects like Le Corbusier and others who professed to be searching for a rational and functional architecture while, to his eyes, merely indulging in irrelevant stylistic manipulations more appropriate to the whims of the fashion industry: "We hear much of designing from the 'inside out' among those who constitute what remains of the architectural profession – that sometimes jolly, sometimes sanctimonious, occasionally chi-chi, and often pathetic organisation of shelter tailors".[4]

With its lightweight, cheap and portable, frame-and-skin construction the Dymaxion House concept actually grew out of the same obsession with the forms of yachts, ships and early aircraft that had inspired Le Corbusier's radical thinking, even though this had led to quite different results. The fact that Fuller was more interested in the prototype than its mass-production possibilities is illustrated by his unwillingness to launch into production for the military market after the war, when orders for his Dymaxion-inspired "Wichita" house looked set to exceed the first 60 000 units the factory was preparing to produce. Fuller's hesitancy may partly have been due to the disastrous debut of his first Dymaxion car, involved in a fatal accident at the gates of the 1933

[4] R. Buckminster Fuller, *Nine Chains to the Moon*, Southern Illinois University Press, Carbondale, 1938 & 1963, p 9.

Chicago World Exposition. The advanced aerodynamics and rear-wheel steering of the car – ineffective at high speeds due to its loss of contact with the ground – were directly inspired by the form of an aeroplane fuselage, confirmed by the famous photograph of one of Fuller's later prototypes of the car, parked on a runway next to his own equally curious-looking aircraft, the amphibious Republic Seabee.[5] A telling example of Fuller's romantic desire to make use of all the most advanced technological possibilities – even where they are not necessarily required or particularly appropriate – comes in his summary of the goals of the Dymaxion project, made in 1983, the year of his death:

> Since I was intent on developing a high-technology dwelling machine that could be air-delivered to any remote, beautiful country site where there might be no roadways or landing fields for airplanes, I decided to try to develop an omni-medium transport vehicle to function in the sky, on negotiable terrain, or on water – to be securely landable anywhere like an eagle.[6]

It is here that Fuller's debt to those first great machine-age poets and romantics, the Italian Futurists, becomes apparent, in his echoing of the infatuation they experienced when confronted with new technological possibilities. As the 1914 manifesto of the group makes clear, while also betraying the provenance of some more recent high-tech preoccupations:

> We must invent and rebuild the Futurist city: it must be like an immense, tumultuous, lively, noble work site, dynamic in all its parts; and the Futurist house must be like an enormous machine. The lifts must not hide like lonely worms in the stair wells; the stairs, become useless, must be done away with and the lifts must climb like serpents of iron and glass up the housefronts.[7]

[5] Reproduced in Martin Pawley, *Buckminster Fuller*, Trefoil Publications, London, 1990, p 81.
[6] R. Buckminster Fuller, quoted in Martin Pawley, *Buckminster Fuller*, Trefoil Publications, London, 1990, p 57.
[7] Sant Elia/Marinetti, "Futurist Architecture", in Ulrich Conrads (ed.), *Programmes and Manifestoes on 20th Century Architecture*, Lund Humphries, London, 1970, p 36.

10 Brinkman and Van der Vlugt – Van Nelle Factory, Rotterdam, 1927–29. (Neil Jackson)

In contrast to Fuller's somewhat blind and deterministic application of new technologies in architecture, Le Corbusier was well aware of the need to mediate between the "raw" engineering of the problems of shelter and the shared cultural expectations of a society in need of reassurance amidst the uncertainties of historical change. For all the latter's rhetoric on the beauty of the great ships, aeroplanes and automobiles in the opening chapters of *Towards a New Architecture*, he also went on to discuss in equivalent detail the architecture of ancient Greece, Rome and the Italian Renaissance. In the section entitled "The Engineer's Aesthetic" he began by claiming that since engineers were "active and useful, balanced and happy in their work", they would soon be monopolising the building process, since: "We no longer have the money to erect historical souvenirs. At the same time, we have got

11 Brinkman and Van der Vlugt – Van Nelle Factory, Rotterdam, 1927–29.
(Neil Jackson)

to wash! Our engineers provide for these things and they will be our
builders."[8]

At the same time he was also anxious to emphasise the unique contribution that the architect must make to the resolution of the design
process, by recovering those abstract formal principles that had been
obscured by the stylistic preoccupations of the "academic" tradition. It
was precisely this tradition, enshrined in the institutionalised teaching
of architecture in France through the influence of the Ecole des Beaux
Arts, that Reyner Banham had blamed for the apparent failure of the
early modernists to deliver on the promise of an authentically machine-
age architecture.

[8] Le Corbusier, *Towards a New Architecture*, translated by Frederick Etchells,
Architectural Press, London, 1946, pp 18–19.

12 Le Corbusier – Villa Savoye, Poissy, Paris, 1929–31. (Alistair Gardner)

This became the dominant theme of his influential book which was highlighted earlier, and his discussion of the Villa Savoye made this notion particularly explicit. By designing a building that merely looked like it was made of new materials and at the same time bore only a formal resemblance to a modern ocean liner – without also possessing a ship's functional rigour or technical sophistication – Le Corbusier had, according to Banham, lapsed back into the kind of traditional symbolic language of metaphor and allusion that the engineer-designers like Fuller appeared to have left behind. What Banham fails to clarify in his assessment of the pre-war architects' achievement is the distinction between two clear lines of development in early modernism which arose from two distinct sources – one from advances in technology and the other from advances in art. Where Banham sees the latter as a distraction from the former, claiming that the: ". . . theorists and designers of the waning twenties cut themselves off not only from their own historical beginnings, but also from their foothold in the world of technology"[9], Le Corbusier presents the alternative view, that the first is

[9] Reyner Banham, *Theory and Design in the First Machine Age*, Architectural Press, London, 1960, p 327.

meaningless without the second and is a part of architecture's larger
responsibility to communicate. As he writes in the chapter on "The
Engineer's Aesthetic":

> Finally, it will be a delight to talk of ARCHITECTURE after so many grain-
> stores, workshops, machines and sky-scrapers. ARCHITECTURE is a thing
> of art, a phenomenon of the emotions, lying outside questions of con-
> struction and beyond them. The purpose of construction is TO MAKE
> THINGS HOLD TOGETHER; of architecture TO MOVE US.[10]

Art and Technology in the Origins of Modernism

Where Banham polarises the debate within modernism, between a
technology-inspired futurism that looks forward to a "golden age" and
a historically-inspired academicism that sees its golden age in the past,
Le Corbusier expresses an alternative possibility. His position relies on
a subtle distinction between a deterministic "machine-architecture"
that is supposed to arise inevitably from the deployment of new technologies, and a properly symbolic "machine-*age*-architecture" which
requires the input of the creative individual to express the aspirations
of the times and thereby takes account of other advances in human
knowledge, in addition to the scientific and the technological. These
would include the developments in painting, literature and music that
were going on at the time – all of which contributed to a profoundly
new way of seeing and understanding the world in the early decades
of the twentieth century. This was a cultural phenomenon in which
architecture should rightly be partaking, as he mentions in a footnote
to the chapter quoted above. He also demonstrates this more explicitly through his own experiments in painting, using many of the techniques developed by the Cubist painters, Picasso and Braque, to
explore the perception of objects in space – inspired in part by Albert
Einstein's contemporary theories of relativity.

[10] Le Corbusier, *Towards a New Architecture*, translated by Frederick Etchells,
Architectural Press, London, 1946, p 23.

A similar confusion as to the true nature of modernist architecture arose from the title of the exhibition which introduced this intially European phenomenon into the architectural scene in North America. "The International Style: Architecture Since 1922", organised by Henry Russell Hitchcock and the architect Philip Johnson at the Museum of Modern Art, New York in 1932, suggested that, far from being a "scientific method" of producing buildings according to the functional and technical requirements of the brief, the new architecture was actually as much a product of the creativity of the individual "artist" as architecture always had been. This conflicting interpretation of the ideals of the Modern Movement had already become apparent in the teaching programme of the Bauhaus – the school set up in Germany as a new model for education, to rival the Classical teaching of the Ecole des Beaux Arts in Paris, but with a technically based curriculum in place of the traditional historical one. Walter Gropius, who directed the new school from its inception in 1919 through to 1928, had attempted to unify the industrial and the creative aspects of the practice of design, through the teaching of architects, artists and sculptors together in the techniques of craft production. Unfortunately, the factional in-fighting between those brought in to teach in the "craftwork" as opposed to the "artwork" sections of the course meant that the school made little headway towards its stated objective of "the creation of standard types for all practical commodities of everyday use . . .".[11]

The emphasis on standardisation for the mass-production market had already caused a rift in the running of another, earlier, group to which Walter Gropius was affiliated, the pre-World War 1 Deutsche Werkbund, for whom he had designed an exhibition pavilion in 1914. In the conference held in Cologne at the time of the exhibition the opposition between the free will of the artist and the determinism of industrial production was made particularly clear in a debate between

[11] Walter Gropius, "Principles of Bauhaus Production", in Ulrich Conrads (ed.), *Programmes and Manifestoes on 20th Century Architecture*, Lund Humphries, London, 1970, p 96.

two of the group's leading voices. Hermann Muthesius, who had recently been in England studying domestic architecture for the German government, set out a series of ten theses on the aims of the Werkbund programme, which were focused on the need for standardisation in design. For example:

> 1. Architecture, and with it the whole area of the Werkbund's activities, is pressing towards standardisation, and only through standardisation can it recover that universal significance which was characteristic of it in times of harmonious culture.

In the second section he went on to claim that standardisation was also the key to an improvement in aesthetic awareness, as it could ". . . alone make possible the development of a universally valid, unfailing good taste."[12] In replying to this presentation, Henry van de Velde, who was also director of the School of Applied Arts in Weimar that later formed the core of the Bauhaus, set out an alternative point of view, even though he was as determined as anyone in the movement at the time to promote such Modernist principles as "truth to materials" and the "honesty" of construction:

> 1. So long as there are still artists in the Werkbund and so long as they exercise some influence on its destiny, they will protest against every suggestion for the establishment of a canon and for standardisation. By his innermost essence the artist is a burning idealist, a free spontaneous creator. Of his own free will he will never subordinate himself to a discipline that imposes upon him a type, a canon.[13]

The final layer in this archeological excavation of the building-as-machine analogy in recent architecture explores this conflict between

---

[12] Muthesius/van de Velde, "Werkbund These and Antitheses" in Ulrich Conrads (ed.), *Programmes and Manifestoes on 20th Century Architecture*, Lund Humphries, London, 1970, p 28.

[13] Muthesius/van de Velde, "Werkbund These and Antitheses" in Ulrich Conrads (ed.), *Programmes and Manifestoes on 20th Century Architecture*, Lund Humphries, London, 1970, p 29.

free will and determinism and reveals its origin in the notion that culture has reached a climax in its historical development. The idea that style had been superseded by functionality and that individual expression no longer had a role in contemporary cultural activity was perhaps most powerfully expressed by Adolf Loos in his 1908 essay entitled *Ornament and Crime*. After a discussion of the relationship between decoration and degeneracy – claiming tattoos and graffiti were both signs of criminality – he went on to suggest how the true indication of cultural advancement and sophistication was the enjoyment of plain, undecorated surfaces. Objects should be free from the trappings of historical style and the encumbrance of irrelevant ornament and he presented this as the conclusion of a potted cultural history:

> A country's culture can be assessed by the extent to which its lavatory walls are smeared. In the child this is a natural phenomenon: his first artistic expression is to scribble erotic symbols on the walls. But what is natural to the Papuan and the child is a symptom of degeneracy in the modern adult. I have made the following discovery and I pass it on to the world: *The evolution of culture is synonymous with the removal of ornament from utilitarian objects.*[14]

While Loos' own architecture indulges in the traditional qualities of marble and stone, it would be the next generation of architects working in concrete, glass and steel who would eventually attempt to generate a truly universal language of functional and utilitarian forms.

The reason these ideas took such firm root in an architectural context in subsequent years has much to do with the philosophical revolution that was underway even before the rise of industrial technology. Even in the sixteenth and seventeenth centuries in Europe the idea of the universe operating as a mechanical device was gaining acceptance in philosophical circles and this in turn stimulated a huge interest in the practice of experimental science. It is this rich heritage of "scientific" philosophy and speculation, together with the idea that history

[14] Adolf Loos, "Ornament and Crime", in Ulrich Conrads, (ed.) *Programmes and Manifestoes on 20th Century Architecture*, Lund Humphries, London, 1970, p 19–20.

might itself be operating as a mechanically developing process, that forms the background to the rise of the machine age in architecture. These ideas paved the way for the eventual assimilation of new technologies into architecture – resolving some of the "confusion" caused by the innovations of the nineteenth century – and it is these ideas that must be considered next in an effort to understand the background to more recent architectural developments.

The Mechanical Universe – Vesalius, Copernicus and Bacon

The two philosophical sources for the dominance of the mechanistic model in twentieth century architecture concern what were traditionally two of the greatest mysteries of the pre-modern world, the first of which is spatial and the second temporal. Probably since the dawn of human consciousness the question of the spatial structure of the physical universe and of the objects found within it has been a source of considerable intrigue and speculation. Much of the world's mythological and religious thinking has addressed the persistent mysteries of why things are the way they are and why they behave in the way they do. By the same token, a similar amount of creative energy has been expended on the question of why some things seem to change with the passage of time while others perpetually appear the same. More recently, however, both science and philosophy have attempted to answer both of these intriguing and fundamental questions by applying a similar model of the mechanistic system – first by considering the universe and its contents as machines and the second by suggesting that history itself follows a mechanical and directed evolution towards a goal.

The first two notable landmarks in the advance of this modern view occured in 1543, when two men produced, completely independently of each other, two remarkably symmetrical innovations. The first, the Italian astronomer Copernicus' book called *On the Revolution of the Planets*, placed the sun, rather than the earth, at the centre of the known universe and thus began a revolution in our understanding of astronomy. The other was the product of a different style of research

– looking "inwards" at the body instead of outwards at the heavens –
and concerned the physical structure and systems of human anatomy.
The Fabric of the Human Body was the work of Andreas Vesalius, the
Flemish physician and anatomist who distrusted the traditional understanding of the workings of the body due to its theoretical derivation
from dissections done on animals. In response to this neglect of a solid
basis in physical fact, Vesalius insisted, like Copernicus had done, on
gathering his own experimental evidence and dismissing all previous
notions born of superstition and speculation.

The most striking aspect of Vesalius' approach to the presentation of
his studies is the mechanical and systematic way in which the components of the body are separated out for inspection. As the skin and the
muscles are stripped away almost violently, the organs and bones
which are revealed by this process are examined independently in isolated illustrations. In spite of the difficulties of obtaining corpses for
dissection, his revolutionary methodology led to significant discoveries
as well as arousing opposition from the Church. It was the same
opposition to "heretical" new practices that Galileo was to encounter
just a few decades later, when he took up the principle of Copernicus'
new universe and confirmed it, to his cost, with his newly acquired
telescope.

With the body as a system divided into its constituent components,
it wasn't long before the forces that animated the resulting "assembly"
also began to yield to a similar kind of mechanical analysis. In 1628,
when William Harvey published his conclusions on the circulation of
the blood due to the pumping action of the heart, the notion of the
body as a mechanical contraption was beginning to take root in
philosophy. The English philosopher and Lord Chancellor Francis
Bacon set out in more formal terminology what he intended would
serve as the basis for a rigorous and systematic experimental science.
In the *Novum Organum* (1620) ("New Instrument; or, True
Directions Concerning the Interpretation of Nature") he established
the approach to scientific investigation that became the foundation of
modern technological advancement. Bacon was frustrated with the
pace of human progress which, to him, was being stifled by its respect

for ancient wisdom. He proposed a new beginning which would start from observation and build up from simple axioms towards more abstract principles. He described this way of working, from the particular towards the general, as an "instrument" for the mind, just like a tool works for the hand. He saw quite clearly the relationship between knowledge and power and felt that nature's mysteries would yield before his methods. He wanted, as he put it in his preface: ". . . to conquer, not an opponent in argument, but Nature herself in action: to seek, in short, not elegant and probable conjectures, but certain and demonstrable knowledge . . .".[15]

Bacon's ideas directly inspired what soon became a widespread preoccupation with research in the sciences and led, in 1660, to the establishment in London of a group called the Royal Society. The institution was set up to support individuals in the pursuit of new knowledge through the process of experiment and many famous figures, including Robert Hooke and Isaac Newton, were involved in the society's pioneering activities. The fact that Christopher Wren was a founder member and president, and that Hooke himself also designed several buildings, makes clear that the early growth of the "profession" of the architect was tied up with the beginnings of science. Even Francis Bacon's work betrays a crossover of ideas, as his essay, *Of Building*, makes clear. The application to useful purposes was his goal for new knowledge, not merely the pleasure of discovery for itself. He extended this principle to his thinking on architecture and came up with a now familiar conclusion: "Houses are built to live in, and not to look on; therefore, let use be preferred to uniformity, except where both may be had."[16]

The Mechanical Mind – René Descartes

What Bacon had achieved for the growth of the sciences in England, René Descartes achieved in France and his *Discourse on Method* and

---

[15] Francis Bacon, *Novum Organum*, Open Court, Chicago, 1994, p 40.
[16] Francis Bacon, *Essays*, J. M. Dent, London, 1994, p 114.

the *Meditations*, published in 1637 and 1641, grew out of a similar reforming objective. Though he was, unlike Bacon, more of a "hands-on" researcher, publishing a collection of works on optics, geometry and meteors, it was his writing on philosophical principles that brought him the widest recognition and assured him of a place in the history of ideas. The full title of the brief and clear summary of his methods – which he wrote in French instead of Latin as a means to popularise his message – was the "Discourse on the Method of Rightly Conducting the Reason and Seeking Truth in the Sciences". Like Bacon, he was intent on providing "instruments" for the mind, to assist in its quest for a clear comprehension of the world, uncompromised by tradition and received conventions. This process involved transcending the body and the messy "confusion" of perceptual experience in order to avoid the "illusions" of the realm of the senses and understand the reality behind mere appearance. His method was to start by questioning his assumptions and reconstructing all knowledge from a foundation of certainty:

> Thus, as our senses deceive us at times, I was ready to suppose that nothing was at all the way our senses represented them to be . . . But I soon noticed that while I thus wished to think everything false, it was necessarily true that I who thought so, was something. Since this truth, *I think therefore I am*, was so firm and assured that all the most extravagant suppositions of the sceptics were unable to shake it, I judged that I could safely accept it as the first principle of the philosophy I was seeking.[17]

It was this clear separation of the reasoning mind from the uncertainties of the crude, "feeling" body that provided Descartes with his starting point for a whole new system of knowledge. The human being, however, is divided in this system, like a pilot steering a ship, and this results in a mechanical conception of the body which is reduced to the level of an automaton. Although Descartes claimed that only animals were in fact true machines, as they lacked any kind of

---

[17] René Descartes, *Discourse on Method*, Bobbs-Merrill, New York, 1956, pp 20–21.

consciousness and freedom of the will, the human body when acting purely by instinct could also be viewed in this mechanistic way:

> When a man in falling thrusts out his hand . . . he does that without his reason counselling him so to act, but merely because the sight of the impending fall penetrating to his brain drives the animal spirits into the nerves in the manner necessary for this motion . . . and as though it were the working of a machine.[18]

This "machine" model of the body was extended to the universe which Descartes concluded could be reduced even further. His principle of mechanism proposed that all phenomena could be explained as the motion of "geometrical matter", where matter, according to his definition is: "susceptible of every sort of division, shape and motion".[19] Descartes held back from publishing his work on astronomy, following Galileo's trial by the church inquisition, and it would take another hundred years or more before the full implications of "Cartesian duality" would be made clear for the body in the most obvious terms. In 1745 and 1748 two books appeared in France that addressed this particular issue. The first, *Man the Machine*, and the second, *Man the Plant*, were written by Julian Offray de La Mettrie, although early editions were anonymously published for fear of provoking a hostile reaction.

The same crossover of ideas that happened in England between the new rigour in science and the growing profession of architecture also took off from Descartes' philosophy in France, through the equivalent of the Royal Society. The French Academy was founded in 1635 and in 1666 it had spawned an Academy of Science. Claude Perrault, who was one of the latter's founder members, was a physician and comparative anatomist by training, although he also, like Robert Hooke, practised architecture as well and built the east façade of the Louvre in Paris,

---

[18] René Descartes, *The Philosophical Works of Descartes*, translated by Elizabeth S. Haldane and G. R. T. Ross, Cambridge University Press, Cambridge, 1967, v2, p 104.
[19] René Descartes, quoted in Anthony Kenny, *Descartes: A Study of his Philosophy*, Thoemmes Press, Bristol, 1997, p 203.

which was completed in 1680. His most memorable work was in architectural theory where he questioned the traditional understanding of number, which had, since Vitruvius in the first century AD, been treated as God-given and of sacred significance. The dimensions of the body were seen as the basis for a system of divinely proportional relationships which, like those in music, would guarantee harmony and ensure that a building would be "in tune" with the universe. This notion of number as the secret to harmony had been revived during the Renaissance but had never been codified and the conflicts that had grown up between rival systems inspired Perrault to resolve the confusion. In his *Ordonnance for the Five Kinds of Columns*, published in 1683, he attempted to set out a once-and-for-all number system, by averaging the dimensions put forward by others. In place of the assumption that proportions were absolute and their recognition an innate capacity of the mind, he reduced the whole question to arbitrary convention, based on learned, rather than any God-given standards. The effect of this shift from the divine to the "convenient" continued the revolution that Descartes had begun. By reducing mathematics from theology to engineering, another "instrument" of comprehension had been created for the mind.

From this grounding in the techniques of spatial description and the mechanistic explanation of natural phenomena came a whole torrent of new "sciences" during the next hundred years. As Michel Foucault has described in his book *The Order of Things*, the eighteenth century saw an expansion in research and classification that went a long way to fulfilling Francis Bacon's great vision. The sciences of botany, geology and paleontology were all born in this period out of the same urge to record and classify. By the end of the century even language and history had begun to be seen as fair game for the sciences, and it is history that proves to be decisive for the progress of the machine-aesthetic in architecture.

The Machine of History – From Vico to Hegel and Viollet-le-Duc

The first landmark in the growth of history as a "scientific" discipline was, ironically, the work of a thinker opposed to the tradition of Cartesian rationality, the Neapolitan philosopher Giambattista Vico. He published his *Principles of a New Science of the Common Nature of Peoples* between 1725 and 1730 with the aims of establishing the value of "poetic wisdom" – which will be considered in Chapter 2 – and at the same time determining a pattern for the development of societies. On the basis that human beings, and not nature, had created cultural institutions and they should therefore be in an ideal position to understand them, he suggested a cyclical system of historical change – from birth to decay and ultimately to re-growth – to explain the discontinuities in the world's great civilisations. It took almost a century before this notional structure was codified into a comprehensive system, which at the same time also established a kind of historical corollary to Descartes' first principle of the self-conscious thinking mind. By presenting Descartes' search for certainty as a historical objective, G. W. F. Hegel in his *Phenomenology of Spirit* placed the reasoning mind at the climax of history, as it reaches the stage of self-understanding through the medium of philosophy. The concept of "Spirit" (or "mind" in some translations) is a force, like a "creator", that uses the world as a vehicle to realise its ultimately philosophical objectives. The objective of Spirit is, according to Hegel, to "know itself as Spirit", as a free, reasoning being, able to understand its own capacities. This awareness has been achieved by a process of historical development, where philosophical insight has gradually grown from confused beginnings to culminate in Hegel's own system of thought. He set out the historical stages through which Spirit passed – in this striving to express itself and thereby come to "know itself" – and, like Vico, he used a cyclical pattern to explain the progression of civilisations. He set up the more abstract – and now famous – dialectical model of thesis, antithesis and synthesis, to explain how the cycles of change in society reflect the different stages of Spirit's developing self-understanding. This historical method of conceiving and of describing his philosophy produces by implication a philosophical conception of history. In his later writings on this subject, where he specifically addresses this historical issue, he also proposes several other significant new concepts.

Besides the influential notion of the "spirit of the age" (or *Zeitgeist*) which grew out of his early philosophy, in the *Phenomenology of Spirit* he also addressed religion and its pivotal role in the development of both architecture and art. In the process of the Spirit's gradual movement towards self-consciousness, religion is seen as an intermediate stage, beyond the primitive's blind struggle for physical survival and prior to the "absolute" knowledge of philosophy and science. Within this stage itself he suggests a division of three phases, beginning with "natural religion" and the worship of landscape features such as mountains, trees and springs. The second is the "religion of art" which belongs to a further phase of development, where societies like the ancient Greeks made images of their Gods, as well as expressing their theology through architecture and ritual. The third phase of religion involves a transcending of the physical world and a movement away from the expression of beliefs embodied in works of art. As Spirit comes to understand itself in a much more abstract way, then religion is believed to be contained in the revelations or "Word" of the Gods. As a further stage in history, science and philosophy then take over, the Spirit in Hegel's system then becomes "transparent" to itself. It no longer needs the support of images to express its understanding, since the tools of abstract thought have taken over in this role. Obviously, in this system the importance of art is reduced, as Hegel claims it is now irrelevant to the course of human progress. He is able to take this "idealist" view by distinguishing between the form of a work of art and its content, or idea, and thereby separating what is symbolised from the medium of its expression. This is a persistent idea in the field of aesthetics, which will come up again in Chapter 2, but which is also important here. By means of this separation Hegel constructs yet another history from within the category of art and based on its various forms. In his lectures on aesthetics given in Berlin in the 1820s Hegel set out in a hierarchical sequence his version of the development of art. From architecture and sculpture, the two most "physical" of media, developed the progressively more abstract disciplines of painting, music and poetry. Whereas the last is the least reliant on sensory stimulation and is capable of expressing the most complex ideas, the first is seen as rather basic and clumsy, and only suitable for the notions of a more primitive culture.

Poetry in its turn must give way to science, as Hegel's relentless progression of reason moves on to explain the world. As the metaphors and allusions give way to hard facts, the process of history is announced as complete. This system consigns architecture to the realm of the distant past and later art historians have had to respond to this troublesome fact. In architecture specifically the reaction has taken two different forms, with the split between engineering and art as a consequence. The key figure in the rise of the architect as engineer is Eugene Emmanuel Viollet-le-Duc, who, writing around 1860, took up Hegel's challenge to the foundations of architecture. As the eclecticism of the time and the debates about style threatened to confirm Hegel's forecast of doom, Viollet set out the case for architecture's continued importance as a technical, rather than an expressive, endeavour. While the nineteenth century revivals of historical styles were partly brought on by Hegel's periodising of history, the confusion that followed had spurred Viollet's search for "timeless" principles, beyond the distractions of symbols and meanings. As he writes, on "Construction" from his *Dictionnaire Raisonné* (anticipating Le Corbusier on the "engineer's aesthetic"):

> The last Romanesque builders, those who after so many attempts had finally dismissed the semi-circular arch, are not visionaries; they do not speculate on the mystical meaning of a curve; they do not know if the pointed arch is more religious than the semi-circular arch; they build – a more difficult task than idle dreaming.[20]

[20] E. E. Viollet-le-Duc, *Rational Building*, translated by George Martin Huss, Macmillan, New York, 1895, p 42.

Like other writers of his time he produced a "universal history" from the origins of architecture in the "primitive hut", but whereas Hegel had been interested in what buildings *meant*, Viollet simply concentrated on how they were *built*. With an emphasis on function and economy of means, all previous architecture was presented as rational – even classical Greek "ornament" was shown to derive from construction. Whereas in his "Lectures" he followed a Hegelian chronology, in the *Dictionnaire* he used a more anatomical method – dividing up his subject into alphabetical sections, more easily, he maintained, to study its parts:

> . . . because this form obliges us, if we might thus say it, to dissect separately in describing the functions performed, the use of each of the diverse parts and of the modifications it has experienced.[21]

Throughout the history of architecture he saw a fundamental principle, in the application of reason to the satisfaction of needs, and this substantiated his case for architecture as a science and saved it from its fate as a historical curiosity. It was this principle which he felt should be applied in his own time, making use of new materials and advances in technology. As he writes in the *Lectures*, again inspired by engineering:

> The constructors of locomotive engines did not take it into their heads to copy a stage-coach team. Moreover we must consider that art is not riveted to certain forms, but that, like human thought, it can incessantly clothe itself in new ones . . . Let us endeavour to proceed thus logically; let us frankly adopt the appliances afforded us by our own times, and apply them without the intervention of traditions which have lost their vitality . . .[22]

---

[21] E. E. Viollet-le-Duc, *The Foundations of Architecture*, translated by Barry Bergdoll and Kenneth D. Whitehead, George Braziller, New York, 1990, p 18.
[22] E. E. Viollet-le-Duc, *Lectures on Architecture*, translated by Benjamin Bucknall, Dover, New York, 1987, v2, p 64–5.

This "renewal" of architecture, based on rational principles, was part of the same search for certainty that Descartes had inaugurated and, in response to Hegel's prognosis of the death of the architect as artist, the engineer had now stepped forward to take over in this role. This was only one aspect of the reaction to Hegel's challenge and another whole tradition will be considered in the following chapter. This will provide an alternative view of architecture and its status as a symbolic activity, with a meaningful place in society within a quite different philosophy of history – questioning the ideology of progress that drives the engine of technological innovation.

Suggestions for further reading

Background

George Basalla, *The Evolution of Technology*, Cambridge University Press, Cambridge, 1988.

René Descartes, *Discourse on Method and The Meditations*, translated by F. E. Sutcliffe, Penguin Books, London, 1968.

G. W. F. Hegel, *Introductory Lectures on Aesthetics*, translated by Bernard Bosanquet, Penguin Books, London, 1993.

G. W. F. Hegel, *Reason in History: A General Introduction to the Philosophy of History*, translated by R. S. Hartman, Library of Liberal Arts, New York, 1953.

Lewis Mumford, *Technics and Civilisation*, Harcourt, Brace, Jovanovich, New York, 1963.

Neil Postman, *Technopoly: The Surrender of Culture to Technology*, Vintage Books, New York, 1993.

Peter Singer, *Hegel*, Oxford University Press, Oxford, 1983.

Foreground

Reyner Banham, *Theory and Design in the First Machine Age*, Architectural Press, London, 1960.

Le Corbusier, *Towards a New Architecture*, translated by Frederick Etchells, Architectural Press, London, 1946.

Viollet-le-Duc, *Lectures on Architecture*, translated by Benjamin Bucknall, Dover, New York, 1987.

Sant'Elia and Marinetti, "Futurist Architecture", in Ulrich Conrads (ed.), *Programmes and Manifestoes on 20th Century Architecture*, Lund Humphries, London, 1970.

Muthesius and van de Velde, "Werkbund These and Antitheses", in Ulrich Conrads (ed.), *Programmes and Manifestoes on 20th Century Architecture*, Lund Humphries, London, 1970.

Richard Rogers, *Architecture: A Modern View*, Thames and Hudson, London, 1990,

Readings

Theodor Adorno, "Functionalism Today", in Neil Leach (ed.), *Rethinking Architecture*, Routledge, London, 1997, pp 6-19.

Peter Buchanan, "Nostalgic Utopia", *Architects Journal*, 4 September/ 1985, pp 60-9.

Adolf Loos, "Ornament and Crime", in Ulrich Conrads (ed.), *Programmes and Manifestoes on 20th Century Architecture*, Lund Humphries, London, 1970, pp 19-24.

Martin Pawley, "Technology Transfer", *Architectural Review*, 9/1987, pp 31-9.

2

Architecture as Art
Aesthetics in Philosophy

The philosophy of history set out in Chapter 1 produced a powerful myth of progress that caused a rift in the culture of architecture. From the view that science will eventually explain all natural phenomena, and new technologies will evolve to cater for all our needs, came the reduction of the design of buildings to a sub-branch of engineering – controlled not by individuals but by economic and physical forces. This deterministic view of architecture, which submits design to a "scientific" methodology was part of a general search for certainty and respectability in the age of reason. From ideas like Viollet-le-Duc's great principle of the application of reason to the satisfaction of needs grew the belief that good buildings would come about "automatically" – providing the requirements were analysed correctly and the appropriate technologies and materials were chosen.

The critique of this "master-narrative" of enlightenment rationality has recently become a major feature of the philosophy of postmodernity. Historically, however, an alternative position can be identified, which supports the status of architecture as a cultural, not merely a technical, activity. The distinction turns on the status of art itself, in a society seemingly dominated by scientific rationality, and involves a questioning of the view that science provides the only "true" description of reality. Art was considered to be redundant in Hegel's system of ideas, because it no longer seemed to contribute to the progression of human knowledge. Likewise, what later became known as "positivism" in both the physical and social sciences – thanks to the French philosopher Auguste Comte – claimed that progress was a steady and linear development involving the gradual accumulation of experimental data that would eventually account for all phenomena within a single unified system. The book that has recently attacked this notion of science and helped restore the case for art as an alternative "language", or means of describing the world, is *The Structure of Scientific Revolutions*. First published in 1962, and written by Thomas Kuhn, a professor of philosophy at Massachusetts Institute of Technology (M.I.T.), the book describes clearly the growth of scientific knowledge, punctuated as it is by periodic upheavals when new innovations are developed. Kuhn sets out an intriguing pattern which appears to recur in the history of science, caused by the appearance of experimental data which fail to fit within an established framework. This framework for interpretation, or "paradigm" as Kuhn prefers to call it, is what controls the scope of research being carried out in a particular period as well as predicting the likely outcome of a range of relevant experiments. This is what Kuhn refers to as the process of *normal science*, which involves the gathering of experimental data in support of a particular paradigm. Gradually this framework is "filled in" with the accumulation of detail, confirming and completing the picture that the paradigm describes in general outline. Any data that falls outside these set parameters can either be ignored as inaccurate or dismissed as irrelevant or, if sufficiently persistent and troublesome for the previous paradigm, can begin to cause misgivings, leading to a "crisis" in the scientific community. In response to this situation an alternative paradigm will be put forward to explain the anomalous data and thereby suggest new areas of research. Those major "paradigm shifts", or *revolutions*, described in the book's title, happen relatively rarely, such as in the Copernican restructuring of the universe or, more recently, with Einsteinian relativity.

The idea of a shared community "language" which undergoes dramatic and regular transformations provides another way of understanding the actual progress of experimental science, beyond the cumulative model of the dominant positivist conception. What Kuhn's description clearly highlights is the importance of the individual who, in the free exercise of their will, can see beyond the dominant paradigm. It is only by questioning received wisdom and the assumptions of tradition that significant breakthroughs have been made which have allowed the expansion of scientific knowledge. While this model borrows from the world of art the idea of changes to our ways of seeing, it also relies on the artist's critical instinct as a means to challenge accepted norms. This notion of the artist as a critic who steps outside the dominant paradigm has also persisted in architecture, as suggested in Chapter 1. To understand the influence of this view of the architect as intuitive artist, it is worth taking a moment to consider the status of art in philosophy - more specifically in aesthetics - both before and after Hegel.

The Origin of Aesthetics – From Plato to Neo-Platonism

In Plato's famous dialogue, *The Republic*, written around 388 BC, the status of art in society was subjected to keen philosophical scrutiny. The problem with art for Plato is its reliance on representation - the copying of objects in nature which are themselves copies of the universal, "ideal" forms. This notion of ideal models arises from Plato's overall ontology, or "philosophy of being", which divides the world into two distinct categories of experience, the "sensible" and the "intelligible" realms. The sensible is the realm we experience, made up of physical and changeable objects, where things are continually in a state of "becoming", as in nature, either growing or decaying. The intelligible realm, on the other hand, contains the "ideas" for the objects in the world, a timeless collection of models which nature can only imperfectly imitate, like the universal letters of the alphabet which can be written down in a variety of ways. The higher realm of forms is itself controlled by a set of geometric and numerical relationships, a notion that Plato inherited from the Greek mathematician Pythagoras. This universal principle of an underlying mathematical or musical harmony is something only the reasoning mind can eventually come to appreciate. The goal for philosophy, according to Plato, was to see beyond all earthly distractions, to leave behind the realm of the senses and to contemplate the unchanging universals. In Book VII of *The Republic*, in the allegory of the cave, Plato constructs an elaborate illustration of this intellectual journey of the philosopher, from the "shadow world" of appearances to the reality and light of true knowledge. Like Hegel's later idealism which builds on similar philosophical assumptions, Plato also has little time for the contribution of the individual artist. He would, as he describes in the final book of *The Republic*, have banished all poets from his ideal well-ordered society, ruled as it was by an enlightened dictatorship of educated "philosopher-kings".

The underlying principles of order and mathematical harmony are the ingredients of Plato's ultimately moralistic brand of aesthetics, which he goes on to describe as part of an ideal educational system:

> And isn't it necessary for the young to be influenced by these qualities everywhere, if they are to do what is truly theirs to do? And these qualities may be seen in everything, in painting, and in ornament, in the making of everything, clothes, buildings, pots . . . and in the forms of living things. In all these, order or good form and its opposite have their places. Things without order, rhythm and harmony go with ill words and ill feelings, but good order goes with courage and self-control.[1]

While Plato is willing to connect beauty to the moral sense of the true and the good – as though the cultivation of good taste would ensure an individual's good behaviour – it is the beauty found in nature more than the work of the mere artist which is the source for this experience and sets the standards of "good design". Usefulness is one factor significant to this quality, which leads to an almost functionalist principle of design:

---

[1] Plato, *The Republic*, translated by I. A. Richards, Cambridge University Press, Cambridge, 1966, Book III (401), p 57.

And for everything – for every sort of instrument, living being, or act – doesn't the question "Is it good, beautiful, or right?" come down to the use it is made for or naturally has?[2]

In the culture of Plato's Greece this appreciation of organic form also inspired an artistic naturalism, particularly in the depiction of the human figure in painting and sculpture. The attempt to express the underlying perfection of the "universal" beneath the "particular" betrays the desire to improve on the "imperfect" versions of the ideal that nature produces. However, all this is directed towards the knowledge of the ideal forms, which only the intellect can ultimately apprehend, concealed as they are beneath the surface of the sensible world. Thus, art in Plato's system is merely the means to an intellectual end, which the philosopher must dispense with in the process of the search for truth.

The ambiguity of the role of art as an improvement of imperfect nature is addressed by Aristotle, Plato's pupil and successor. In the Platonic system nature provides an "image" of the underlying forms whereas art, as an image of nature, is even further removed from truth. Aristotle's philosophy ends up reversing this arrangement, suggesting that art can, by perfecting nature, lead us closer to the truth. For Aristotle reality lies not in the realm of being – Plato's timeless realm of forms – but in the empirical reality of experience, of sensible objects which grow and decay. By starting with the objects of sensory experience he developed an alternative brand of "normative" idealism. His definition of "universals" was based on the averaging of "particulars": by studying numerous individuals one could define the nature of the "ideal". This study of the particular that Aristotle recommends becomes important also for his philosophy of art. Though he wrote mostly of literature, including poetry and drama, he recommends the arts as a source of practical knowledge in the way that Plato never did. Where Plato talked of abstract notions such as goodness and truth, Aristotle is concerned with practical issues of emotion and behaviour. In *The*

---

[2] Plato, *The Republic*, translated by I. A. Richards, Cambridge University Press, Cambridge, 1966, Book X (601), p 178.

Poetics he set out a lot of practical advice, covering the construction of plots and dramatic characters for the theatre. Throughout he is concerned with his potential to educate an audience through the actions of the performers dealing with moral dilemmas. The experience of catharsis – the emotional release of shared experience – is described as a major effect of tragic drama in the theatre. It is this ability of the audience to empathise with the characters' emotions that becomes the standard for all art, whether musical or visual. This notion that art offers a heightening of experience became a powerful force in later thinking on aesthetics. As Aristotle writes in *The Poetics*, it allows an approach to the universal beyond that provided by the "imperfect" individual:

> As tragedy is an imitation of personages better than the ordinary man, we should follow the example of good portrait-painters, who reproduce the distinctive features of a man, and at the same time, without losing the likeness, make him handsomer than he is.[3]

When Aristotle writes of beauty in the more abstract sense, he cites order and harmony as its fundamental components. Like Plato, he looks to nature for examples of these qualities, but he concentrates on physical causes rather than metaphysical models. He proposed an inner force to explain the functioning of living organisms, as well as the cause-and-effect principle, which would influence later thinking in science. Where Plato tried to show the emergence of the particular from the universal, Aristotle reversed this movement with his normative ideals. Similarly, in Plato, the artist seems trapped by the universals and restricted to the imitation of the forms found in nature. In Aristotle, however, the individual has some freedom to discover, like the scientist, new ideals in the world. The opposition set up here between the two views of the artist became part of a dichotomy between two systems of thought. From Plato's idealism and the dominance of the intellect came the Rationalist tradition of Descartes, Hegel and others. On the other hand, from Aristotle came an emphasis on the

---

[3]   Aristotle, *The Poetics*, translated by I. Bywater, Princeton University Press, Princeton, 1984, 1454b, p 2327.

senses and the empirical philosophies of Locke, Berkeley and Hume. Before approaching this debate and its consequences for aesthetics, another figure must be considered as an early contributor to this field.

The Roman philosopher Plotinus, who lived in the third century AD, managed to resolve some of the contradictions between the two philosophies set out above. In developing a complete system from Plato's fragmented dialogues, he produced an influential aesthetic theory as a component of his neo-Platonism. Beginning with Plato's divine creator as the ultimate source of truth and beauty, Plotinus set up a hierarchical system to explain the relationship between different levels of being. These levels are described as emanations from the "One" – the "Absolute" source of the order of the world. From the One comes the divine mind, which Plotinus called Nous, and from this comes the Soul, both of the world and of individuals. The Soul, as for Plato, controls or pilots the body, which is part of the final emanation into the physical world of objects. All levels partake of the divine order of the One, and it is this order that the Soul comes to recognise in its contemplation of beauty. Individual beauty is therefore a symbol of an underlying cosmic harmony, which the Soul can perceive because of its relationship with the One. This higher form of beauty is what the individual soul aspires to, and the artist therefore has this goal in mind. In nature this beauty is only imperfectly represented whereas the artist can discover it more directly from within. It is here that Plotinus parts company with Plato's thinking, as the artist is given a privileged role in his system:

> Still the arts are not to be slighted on the ground that they create by imitation of natural objects; for, to begin with, these natural objects are themselves imitations; then, we must recognise that they give no bare reproduction of the thing seen but go back to the Reason-Principles [Ideas] from which nature itself derives, and furthermore, that much of their work is all their own; they are holders of beauty and add where nature is lacking.[4]

---

[4] Plotinus, *Enneads*, translated by Stephen MacKenna, Penguin Books, London, 1991, V, viii, 1, p 411.

This notion of the artist having access to divine harmony became a powerful notion for later thinking in aesthetics. Besides the question of the status of art as a "unique" form of knowledge – the issue of whether philosophy could ever replace aesthetic experience – it is here also where the later debate between the Classical and the Romantic has its roots, in the arguments over the role of the artist. In the Classical tradition the artist is constrained by historical precedent, which acts as a repository of the timeless ideal forms. Romanticism, on the other hand, holds the creative individual to be supreme, with the artist as a "genius" inventing freely from within. Of course, within both traditions art may still be seen as subservient to rationality, and it is this question which forms the background to the debates going on in aesthetics today. Before addressing these more contemporary issues and their implications for the theory of architecture, there are two other contributions from the history of aesthetics which should be briefly considered. The first is from the Renaissance and the revival of Classical ideas and the second happens in the eighteenth century and provides the background to the rise of Romanticism.

The Renaissance is so called due to the rebirth of Classical ideas, whose influence spread rapidly thanks in part to the new technique of printing text from moveable type.[5] After Gutenberg's famous Bible appeared in 1456, a proliferation of printed books appeared during the following hundred years. In addition to the new editions of Vitruvius' ten books on architecture, written originally at the height of the Roman Empire, in the first century AD, the writings of the ancient philosophers were also subjected to reinterpretation. In both instances an aesthetic doctrine was developed around the notion of a universal harmony and in both the definition of beauty was based on intellectual rather than physical qualities. This was evident in the commentary on Plato's *Symposium* written by Marsilio Ficino in 1475, although it was in a letter to his friend Cavalcanti that Ficino best sums up the basic principles of the period's Platonic preoccupations:

[5]   In fact moveable type had been used in China since the eleventh century AD. See George Basalla, *The Evolution of Technology*, Cambridge University Press, Cambridge, 1988, p 169–95.

The beauty of bodies does not consist in the shadow of materiality, but in the clarity and gracefulness of form, not in the hidden bulk, but in a kind of luminous harmony, not in an inert and stupid weight, but in a fitting number and measure. Light, gracefulness, proportion, number and measure, which we apprehend by thought, vision and hearing.[6]

The architects of the Renaissance tried to demonstrate these principles in the many depictions of the famous "Vitruvian" figure. With arms extended in a "crucified" posture the body would usually be shown inside a circle and a square. Leonardo da Vinci produced perhaps the most memorable version, although Cesariano and Francesco di Giorgio both used a similar illustration (see Figure 1 below). The link was the notion of a set of timeless ordering principles, which Vitruvius had maintained could be discovered in the architecture of the ancients. As he described it himself, in the chapter on the layout of temples:

Therefore if it is agreed that number is found from the articulation of the body, and that there is a correspondence of the fixed ratio of the separate members to the general form of the body, it remains that we take up those writers who in planning the temples of the immortal gods so ordained the parts of the work that, by the help of proportion and symmetry, their several and general distribution is rendered congruous.[7]

By the time the model of the Renaissance treatise was first imitated in England, in the shape of Henry Wotton's book *The Elements of Architecture* (1624), the harmonic correspondence between the body and the cosmos had also appeared in the writings of the metaphysical poets. George Herbert in particular, in his poem "Man", described an identical fascination with harmony and proportion:

---

[6] Marsilio Ficino, letter to Giovanni Cavalcanti, quoted in Albert Hofstadter and Richard Kuhns (eds), *Philosophies of Art and Beauty*, University of Chicago Press, Chicago, 1964, p 204.
[7] Vitruvius, *On Architecture*, translated by Frank Granger, Harvard University Press, Cambridge, 1983, Book III, Ch. I, p 165–7.

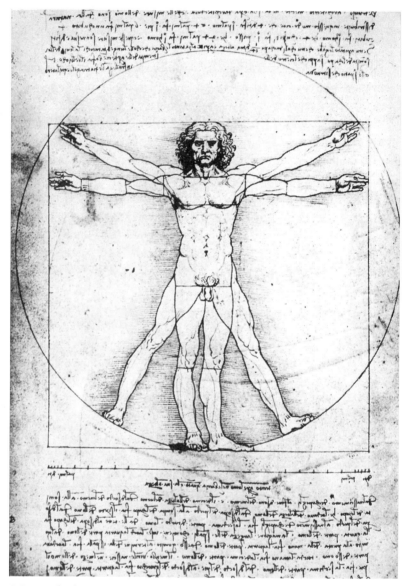

1 Leonardo da Vinci – "Vitruvian" figure, c. 1500.

Man is all simmetry
Full of Proportions, one Limme to another,
And all to all the world besides:
Each Part may call the furthest, Brother:
For Head with Foot hath private Amitie,
And both with Moones and Tides.[8]

George Herbert died in 1633, the year that Galileo was tried for heresy by the Church and the same year that Descartes had abandoned his plans for an ambitious treatise entitled *The World*. The world was, however, rapidly changing, with the rise of the new sciences mentioned in Chapter 1. It was in response to these developments towards the end of the seventeenth century that the philosophy of Plato was once again reassessed. The signs of impending acceleration in the growth of technology, as well as the philosophical trend towards the construction of "systems", was met in England by opposition from various Neoplatonic philosophers – most notably, in the final decade of the century, by Anthony Ashley Cooper, the third Earl of Shaftesbury. For Shaftesbury, the focus of aesthetic investigation was also directed towards the beauty of nature, particularly the relationship set out in Plato's philosophy between the true, the beautiful and the good. As he wrote in the first volume of his *Characteristics*, published originally in 1711:

> For all beauty is truth. True features make the beauty of a face; and true proportions the beauty of architecture; as true measures that of harmony and music. In poetry, which is all fable, truth still is the perfection.[9]

While this statement reiterates the Renaissance view of the divine origins of underlying order, Shaftesbury is actually more concerned with the effect of beauty on the mind of the observer. He considers the contemplation of a beautiful object to be a creative act in its own right, as the sensibility towards the quality of beauty is being "constructed"

---

[8] George Herbert, "Man", quoted in Joseph Rykwert, *The Dancing Column: On Order in Architecture*, MIT Press, Cambridge, MA, 1996, p v.

[9] Shaftesbury, *Characteristics*, quoted in Albert Hofstadter and Richard Kuhns (eds), *Philosophies of Art and Beauty*, University of Chicago Press, Chicago, 1964, p 241.

by the individual's experience. It is this interest in the psychology of beauty and the process of aesthetic experience that set the pattern for the work on aesthetics within the British Empiricist tradition.

The Empiricists believed that knowledge derived directly from the senses, that ideas were built up out of the sense-data of experience. This contrasts with the view of the European Rationalists, like Descartes who, as described in Chapter 1, thought sense experience unreliable and began with the innate capacities of the disembodied intellect. It was only later in the eighteenth century, in the work of the German philosopher Immanuel Kant, that a resolution of these two positions produced another significant advance in the history of aesthetic thinking. In the meantime the term "aesthetics" had been coined, in the writing of another German called Alexander Baumgarten. He derived the word from the Greek *Aisthesis*, meaning sensory perception, betraying the influence of the Empiricist preoccupation with knowledge based on experience. In fact there was at this time a crossover between British and German philosophy through the influence of Shaftesbury and his successors, Hutcheson and Burke. Edmund Burke is perhaps most noteworthy for his idea of the sublime, which he formulated in opposition to the concept of the beautiful. He proposed these as two separate categories of aesthetic experience and he also described them in psychological terms. In all these developments the emphasis is shifting – from the *object* to the *subject* of aesthetic experience. Instead of seeing art as simply a means to an intellectual end, where beauty merely provides an image of the underlying principles of order and perfection, the new ideas suggested that art provided a unique form of "knowledge", a realm of specifically sensory awareness which could not be obtained by any other means.

The Aesthetics of "Genius" – From Kant to Nietzsche

It was Kant who perhaps most famously pursued this intriguing insight, incorporating the notion of aesthetic judgement into his overall philosophical system. Kant's first two great critiques covering what he called "pure" and "practical" reason dealt in turn with the problem of knowledge and then with the question of morality. The aesthetic function according to Kant was part of the general faculty of judgement, which he then described in his third critique as being the mediator between the other two. This third work was itself divided into two distinct sections, with the second half dealing with judgements based on purpose, or "teleology". The first half, by contrast, dealt with the opposite situation, where aesthetic judgements are made which are independent of purpose. This was one of Kant's main principles in his definition of the *beautiful* which he claims consists of a kind of "purposiveness without purpose".[10] Nature again became the model for the judgement of beauty in art, where the object is seen as having its own inner purpose. This is as distinct from being a means to an end and involves the independence of the artwork from any use by the observer. These are just some of the tests as to the nature of the aesthetic, which Kant attempted to establish as a kind of autonomous realm. Another of his claims which exerted a long-lasting influence was the idea that beautiful art was the product of inspired genius. He described the culmination of ideas already hinted at above, that art was essentially about invention rather than the imitation of models. This suggests the transcendence of traditional Classical principles and prepares the way for the Romantic movement in the decades to follow:

> We thus see that genius is a *talent* for producing that for which no definite rule can be given; it is not a mere aptitude for what can be learned by a rule. Hence *originality* must be its first property.[11]

The aesthetic idea that is the original product of the creative artist is the key to art's claim that it provides a unique brand of knowledge. While technical skills can be passed on and art can be discussed in ordinary language, the artistic idea in itself can never be expressed in any other way. It is perhaps on this particular point that Kant's

---

[10] Immanuel Kant, *Critique of Judgement*, translated by J. H. Bernard, Hafner Press, New York, 1951, §17, p 73.

[11] Immanuel Kant, *Critique of Judgement*, translated by J. H. Bernard, Hafner Press, New York, 1951, §46, p 150.

thinking remains most distinct from Hegel, who just a decade or so later developed his alternative views of art. Where Hegel had tried to separate the aesthetic idea from the form of the art-object, as a means of consigning artistic practice to its lowly place in his philosophy, Kant and the Romantics after him had insisted on their inseparable unity and established the alternative view of the continued relevance of "aesthetic knowledge".

Where Hegel describes the history of philosophy as a continual progress towards "absolute knowing", he downgrades the role of the artist to that of a redundant supporting actor. Where art once had a useful function in the primitive stages of cultural development, it was then rendered obsolete by the superior precision of philosophical thinking. This "scientific" view of the growth of knowledge, which proposed that all life's mysteries would eventually be solved, ignores the function of art as a mode of understanding and a necessary vehicle for critical debate. This notion of art as a means of criticism - a way of diverging from the dominant "paradigms" - is a vital legacy of the Romantic revolution in early nineteenth century literature and art. The Romantics attacked the notion of authority and the idea that one could discover the true nature of things. They dismissed the possibility of objective knowledge about the world and instead promoted individual expression. Their frustration grew, to a large extent, from the current dominance of scientific rationality which reduced the richness of experience to the dry descriptions of scientific formulae. Goethe's meditations on the beauty of a dragonfly in the *Leipzig Song Book* provide a perfect illustration of the poet's predicament:

> . . . It flits and hovers, resting not –
> Hush! On a willow bough it lights;
> I have it in my fingers caught,
> And now I seek its colours true,
> And find a melancholy blue –
> Such is thy lot, dissector of delights![12]

[12] Johann Wolfgang von Goethe, from the *Leipzig Song Book*, quoted in Ernst Cassirer, *The Philosophy of the Enlightenment*, Princeton University Press, Princeton, 1951, pp 344–5.

The target of Goethe's poem is the reductivist tendency of scientific fact, the loss of the qualitative grasp of things that the work of art is able to provide. We "murder to dissect", as Wordsworth wrote, summing up the prevailing outlook, where the process of anatomical dissection had become the paradigm for all forms of knowledge (see Figure 2). By contrast, the nineteenth century saw a series of reactions to this position, where philosophers attempted to support the claims for the contribution of the creative artist. Arthur Schopenhauer, responding to Hegel, proposed that the world was indeed driven by an energising force – where this differed from Hegel's "spirit" was in the manner of its highest expression, which according to Schopenhauer was neither philosophy nor science. He in fact saw the work of art as the highest expression of human consciousness, being more universal, and hence more powerful, than the fragmentary "dissections" of rational concepts. A fellow German, Friedrich Nietzsche, writing in the second half of the nineteenth century, produced a similarly powerful critique of the dominance of logic and rationality. In his later work he was to call for a "revaluation of all values", as they had been handed down by tradition within the Western intellectual canon. The basis for this call came from his suspicion of the dominance of science, which he regarded as a form of illusion, as he did both philosophy and art.

In *The Birth of Tragedy* (1872), Nietzsche made a study of Greek theatre and its origins in the "spirit of music". In the period prior to the systematic philosophy which began with Socrates in the pages of Plato, he detected a high point of cultural expression in the manner that Hegel had done before him. In the best of Greek tragic drama he sensed the resolution of contrary forces – the rational and emotional tendencies symbolised by the deities Apollo and Dionysus. What happens with the rise of philosophy is the separation of these two traditions, as the Apollonian tendency dominates, with its emphasis on intelligibility:

> Socrates is the archetype of the theoretical optimist who, in his faith in the explicability of the nature of things, attributes the power of a panacea to knowledge and science, and sees error as the embodiment of evil.[13]

[13] Friedrich Nietzsche, *The Birth of Tragedy*, translated by Shaun Whiteside, Penguin Books, London, 1993, p 74.

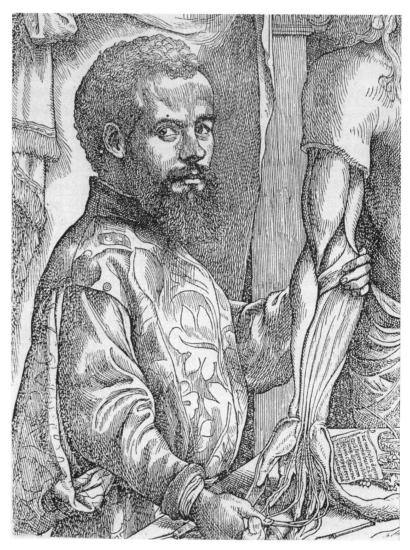

2 Andreas Vesalius – Dissected arm, woodcut from *De Humani Corporis Fabrica*, 1543.

As part of this rationalising process, the *beautiful* was defined in terms of the *intelligible*, with drama dismissed as irrational and even dangerous for "susceptible souls". The limits of this "traditional" philosophy were Nietzsche's real and abiding interest, and in this he echoed the Romantics before him, as well as anticipating many more recent debates. He was against the idea that science expressed the truth about an "objective" world and he made a claim for the continued importance of the artist, when he questioned the very limits of logic itself:

> Might there be a realm of wisdom from which the logician is excluded? Might art even be a necessary correlative and supplement to science?[14]

Aesthetics and Deconstruction – From Heidegger to Derrida

This notion of the limits of science resurfaces again in the twentieth century, in a debate on the status of art which is still influential in philosophy today. The main protagonists in this debate are, again, two German philosophers, Martin Heidegger and Ernst Cassirer, who represent two distinct traditions. Both philosophers wrote on the subject of art as a form of knowledge, but their conclusions on the relationship between art and philosophy differed widely. Heidegger's work has proved to be the more influential, due in part to its breadth and scope, as he set out to develop a new grounding for ontology – or philosophy of being – and, like Nietzsche, he tried to deconstruct its long-held traditions. He attempted to see beyond the limitations of language by examining other forms of expression. His writings on poetry, technology and art suggest they all have a significant function: by revealing the presence of truth in the world, they provide an insight into the mystery of "Being". This *Being* is the great theme running throughout

---

[14] Friedrich Nietzsche, *The Birth of Tragedy*, translated by Shaun Whiteside, Penguin Books, London, 1993, p 71.

Heidegger's work and it is here that he departs from Cassirer and shows his adherence to the philosophy of Hegel. Being is not an entity as such but an underlying force, like Hegel's Spirit, and it manifests itself in the work of art much more distinctly than in everyday objects. This idea that art "condenses" reality into a truer representation of Being echoes Aristotle's view that the artist must idealise the individual, in order to attempt to produce an image of the universal from the particular. When Heidegger discusses this, in the essay called *The Origin of the Work of Art*, written in the 1930s but not published until 1950, he describes it as a process of revealing a world that is implied within the work itself. The famous example that he describes, of a van Gogh painting of a peasant's shoes, provides an illustration of the kind of truth that he felt a work of art was able to express. By suggesting a larger context around or behind the particular object, such as the life of the peasant farmer which can be inferred from the depiction of the shoes, the work of art can reveal a world in an immediate and powerful way. Heidegger describes this in a lyrical language, bordering on poetry itself, as he does in the example of the Greek temple which he considers from a similar point of view. The temple, he says, depicts nothing: it merely stands there in its "rock-cleft valley", while at the same time it implies a set of ritual activities and thereby conjures up a way of life.

The power of man-made objects to carry stories in this direct way has many lessons for the designer of buildings, which we will return to in the next chapter. The work of art, however, remains subordinate to the work of language, which Heidegger continually comes back to in all his analyses of forms of expression. It is here that he echoes Hegel in the priority he gives to philosophy, with language supposedly being the true medium of thought and, in Heidegger's system, the "house of Being". It is language that acts for Heidegger as a repository of the history of Being, and he often uses etymology to uncover a word's hidden primal meanings. In another sense language is primary, according to Heidegger's scale of priorities, in that language exists as a system prior to any individual's attempts to make use of it. This idea that "language speaks man" – rather than man speaking language – reveals a deter-

ministic tendency in his thought that appears to limit individual freedom. This acquiescence to a kind of "historical destiny" proved to be
troubling for later critics, as did Heidegger's support for German
nationalism during the 1930s and beyond.

Where Heidegger's search for the "truth" of Being led him, like
Hegel, to favour poetry and language, Ernst Cassirer, on the other
hand, began from a different set of assumptions and this led him to
an alternative conclusion. Cassirer sidestepped the metaphysical
questions of Heidegger's philosophy of Being and instead took up the
problem of knowledge. It was this more than anything that caused
their difference of opinion which Heidegger expressed in a review of
Cassirer's work. By dealing with epistemology as distinct from ontology, Cassirer was following in the footsteps of Kant, who, as we saw
earlier, had produced the three great critiques which each dealt with
one aspect of knowledge. Kant's critiques or enquiries into the "conditions of possibility" under which we could know anything about the
world had produced the distinction between the real world and the
world which we know in our minds. The distinction turns on the fact
that what we know about the world is limited by the capacity of our
brains, which are structured in such a way as to "frame" our perceptions to fit into certain pre-given forms. As these perceptions depend
on schema like three-dimensional space and time, Kant made it clear
that our knowledge is restricted by these different categories or forms
of thought. Cassirer picked up on this principle to develop a theory of
knowledge, based on the variety of what he called "symbolic forms",
and in the process he modified the chronological sequence set out in
Hegel's history of aesthetics.

Where Hegel presented philosophy as the highest achievement of
human knowledge, with art as a primitive phase now past its useful
purpose, Cassirer allowed all media an equivalent importance in that
each has a unique role to play. He did this by considering the origins
of language in the assignment of symbols to objects and then extend-
ing this metaphorical basis of all language systems to the analysis of
symbolism in art. If art could be said to function as another form of
language, or another means of describing the world, then whole disci-

plines like history, philosophy and science could also be seen as languages in themselves. In the *Philosophy of Symbolic Forms* published in three volumes in the 1920s, he set out the basic principles of this theory, but it was only with his later publication, his *Essay on Man*, that he applied them to this much broader field. This general study of linguistics in other fields of cultural expression will be developed further in the following two chapters where the language model is considered in detail. In the more recent theories of architecture this notion has been widely influential, whether inspiring strong allegiance or provoking opposition.

For our present study the major impact of this kind of relativism between languages has been the challenge to the domination of science as the only true description of reality. By questioning the objectivity of science and its claims to the source of truth, Cassirer helped to reinstate the importance of other ways of describing the world. Another philosopher, Ludwig Wittgenstein, who was writing around the same time, came to a similar realisation about languages in the course of his own research. Having begun by searching for a pure language based on logical and mathematical principles, he ended up by abandoning this and devising the notion of "language-games". His conclusion was that no single language – however precise it might be – could ever give a total and accurate description of the world. As each mode of expression has its own range of uses, a composite picture is built up from the overlapping of these various discourses. Each one makes its own contribution towards our overall knowledge of the world.

The reassessments of science by Thomas Kuhn and other writers, which were discussed at the beginning of this chapter, should also be compared with the reassessment of philosophy and its similar purported claims to a kind of objectivity. The techniques of deconstructing the inherited traditions of Western philosophy, to overcome the limitations of this dominant model of rationality, have become popular in philosophy in the last several decades, though the process has been attempted in different ways in the past. As we saw earlier with the Romantic movement, there was a similar critique of a dominant "paradigm" and the freedom that resulted from this has expanded the boundaries of human knowledge. Martin Heidegger, in a similar vein, also challenged the assumptions of philosophy and attempted what he called a "critical un-building" of its traditions. It was this notion that was picked up by the French philosopher Jacques Derrida when he coined the term "deconstruction" to describe his own approach to the problem.

In Derrida's work one could say that philosophy is being done, if not "with a hammer" – as Nietzsche recommended – then at least with a crow-bar, for the purpose of opening up and revealing. Much of his writing deals specifically with the work of previous philosophers, as he attempts to expose their initial assumptions and to question their conclusions. He often does this through a process of re-enacting their own thinking and thereby revealing the fragile logic of many common philosophical principles. His goal is not a nihilistic one of simply attacking and destroying, although he has often been lambasted for seeming to disparage the achievements of philosophy. As he says in an interview, on the general outlook of his thinking:

> To 'deconstruct' philosophy, thus, would be to think – in the most faithful, interior way – the structured genealogy of philosophy's concepts, but at the same time to determine – from a certain exterior that is unqualifiable or unnameable by philosophy – what this history has been able to dissimulate or forbid, making itself into a history by means of this somewhere motivated repression.[15]

To help escape from this repression Derrida writes in a complex manner, using an often dense and poetic language, which suggests the "exterior" realm he referred to above. In this approach he again follows Heidegger, in his similar use of poetic language, and it is this crossing over of literary genres that has allowed him to step outside the conventions of his field. It is this style of presenting his thoughts that has attracted criticism from "analytical" philosophers, those who still

---

[15] Jacques Derrida, *Positions*, translated by Alan Bass, University of Chicago Press, Chicago, 1981, p 6.

adhere to the principles of Positivism – such as those with which Wittgenstein began and soon abandoned.

Derrida is likewise concerned with the limits of language, together with the general principles and mechanisms of signification, and in this he takes off from the ideas of Structuralism, which we will return to in Chapter 4. In his preoccupation with language as the very medium of philosophy, he betrays a similar priority to Heidegger, although he is much more concerned with the peculiarities of writing as distinct from the traditional emphasis on speech. The difference is significant for much of Derrida's work but what is important here is the wider objective – by enquiring into the medium of his discipline with such vigour he set a pattern which has inspired others to follow. In architecture his ideas have found an enthusiastic reception, especially among those looking to challenge historical tradition. His frequent use of metaphors drawn from architectural sources has also been the source of much direct inspiration. Despite the problems with applying the process of design what began as a tool for analysis, Derrida has collaborated with the architect Peter Eisenman with some success, and we will return to this theme later in concluding this chapter.

Another source of new ideas that have crossed over into architecture is the philosophy of Gilles Deleuze and his collaborator Felix Guattari. They too have focused on language as a theme in much of their work, including the multiplicity of possible "language-games" as ways of conceiving and describing the world. This pragmatic theme of potential usefulness, as opposed to the "truth-value" of various languages, also forms part of Deleuze's general vision of theory as a "box of tools". In his early work he uses the theories of individual philosophers from the past to form a hybrid with his own thoughts through a process of dynamic reinterpretation. The resulting offspring of these relationships provides a model of his later theory, where he sets out the general strategy of adopting "voices" for different purposes. In all of this, as with Derrida, there is a lesson for other disciplines, as their creative engagement with the past provides a means to deal with the problems of tradition. More importantly for the theory of architecture, their work suggests other interpretive possibilities, such as the recovery and reassessment of previously marginal works of architecture.

Architecture and the Housing of Tradition

In architecture the debate over the truth-value of different languages has also been influential in the development of modernism. As the argument between Muthesius and van de Velde made clear, the role of the artist in architecture has often been questioned. In the early years of modern architecture a division had developed between the deterministic methods of science and the free inventions of the artist. The architects of the expressionist wing of modernism, such as Erich Mendelsohn and Hans Scharoun, had demonstrated early on that they were more inspired by the vision of painters. Experiments with the multiple viewpoints of the Cubist artists Picasso and Braque were reflected in the fragmented geometries of buildings by Scharoun and Le Corbusier. The sculptural forms of Mendelsohn's Einstein Tower also provide an intriguing and paradoxical example, showing the influence of scientific theories without the blind application of new technology. The tower as built is a hybrid of traditional and modern construction, with a frame of reinforced concrete and an infill of brick and stucco. This produces a striking visual image of a universe in motion, like the atomic model of physical matter as well as the Cubist canvasses mentioned above. This notion of the capacity of architecture to express a narrative in a spatial language is again echoed in the Dutch De Stijl movement as well as many later projects by Le Corbusier. The attempt to subordinate the expression of technology in order to achieve a sculptural quality in space and form became a dominant trait of several large-scale projects built in the period after World War 2. While the bird-like profile of Eero Saarinen's TWA Terminal caused a stir, perhaps the most famous of these projects is the Sydney Opera House, designed by the Danish architect Jorn Utzon. The Opera House, completed in 1973, won in a competition in 1956, the same year as

3 Le Corbusier – Pilgrimage Chapel, Ronchamp, Belfort, 1950–55. (Alistair Gardner)

Scharoun's major project for the Berlin Philharmonie. Both buildings have become icons for their respective host cities, despite the technical problems of building them and the functional challenges of inhabiting them. A more recent example of this phenomenon is Frank Gehry's Guggenheim museum, completed recently in the run-down and neglected Spanish city of Bilbao. This building's complexity provides a startling demonstration of the advances in information technology, as the hand-crafted models, made in the architect's own office, have been computerised into digital data and transferred directly into the construction process. Another project which promises to update a city's image is Daniel Libeskind's extension to the Victoria and Albert Museum in London. This spiral of "distorted boxes" offers a challenge to its conservative context and should, perhaps almost incidentally, provide an intriguing series of exhibition spaces. On a smaller scale,

4 Erich Mendelsohn – Einstein Tower, Potsdam, 1917–21. (Alistair Gardner)

5 Eero Saarinen – TWA Terminal, JFK Airport, New York, 1956–62. (Alistair Gardner)

this principle of heightening awareness of context through the contrast of old and new, is made visible in the most dramatic fashion in a rooftop building in the centre of Vienna. The design by Coop Himmelblau for a suite of offices and conference space displays a blatant disregard for structural logic or conventional townscape principles. Having dispensed with the common-sense solution, the building suggests a deeper agenda and the result of its fragmented geometry is the questioning of the city's traditional homogeneity. What all these projects show is the power of a sculptural, spatial language – one which cannot be explained away or easily justified in rational terms. These are all buildings that capture the imagination and inspire the user to new experiences, and they all work by disrupting assumptions about conventional functional and contextual requirements.

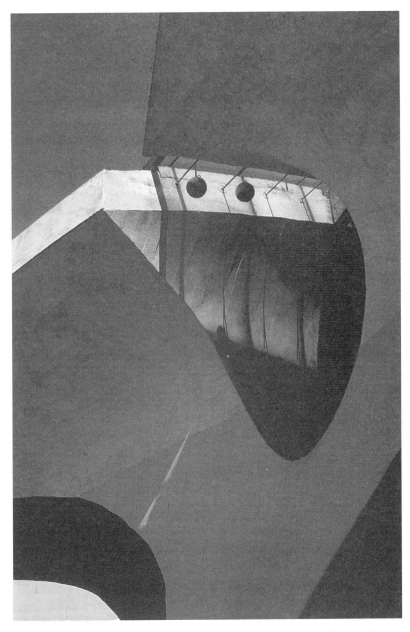

6 Eero Saarinen – TWA Terminal, JFK Airport, New York, 1956–62. (Alistair Gardner)

7 Jorn Utzon – Sydney Opera House, Sydney, Australia, 1957–73. (Neil Jackson)

8 Hans Scharoun – Philharmonie and Chamber Music Hall, Berlin, 1956–87. (Neil Jackson)

9 Renzo Piano Building Workshop – Museum of Science and Technology, ("New Metropolis"), Amsterdam, 1992–97 (Jonathan Hale)

10 Frank O. Gehry – Guggenheim Museum, Bilbao, 1991–97. (Neil Leach)

11 Frank O. Gehry – Guggenheim Museum, Bilbao, 1991–97. (Neil Leach)

12 Frank O. Gehry – Loyola Law School, Los Angeles, California, 1981–84. (Neil Jackson)

13 Daniel Libeskind – Extension to Victoria and Albert Museum (project), London, 1998. (Andrew Putler)

Much recent work in this direction has referred specifically to the philosophy of deconstruction, as inspiration for this kind of challenge to tradition and expectation. Particularly interesting in this regard is the collaboration between Derrida and Peter Eisenman, after he had been invited by the architect to work with him on a portion of the Parc de la Villette in Paris. The most startling aspect of this project for the purpose of our current discussion is the analysis that Derrida makes of the plans for the larger project. By taking up the themes of Bernard Tschumi's masterplan, he effectively reads his own philosophy into the architectural forms proposed. In the essay "Point de Folie – maintenant de l'architecture" he sets up an intriguing scenario where Tschumi's

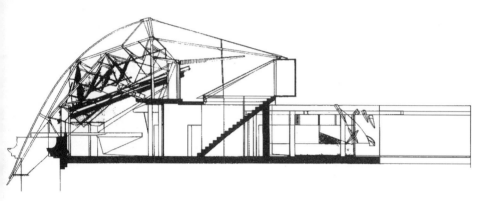

14 Coop Himmelblau – Rooftop remodelling, Vienna, 1983–88. (Redrawn by the author after Coop Himmelblau)

15 Bernard Tschumi – Parc de la Villette, Paris, 1982–91. (Jonathan Hale)

16 Bernard Tschumi – Parc de la Villette, Paris, 1982–91. (Jonathan Hale)

series of "follies", or pavilions in the park, come to represent the kind of philosophy that Derrida himself is actually searching for. As he writes of the follies' challenge to the conventional norms of the discipline of architecture:

> The *folies* put into operation a general dislocation; they draw into it everything that, until *maintenant* [now], seems to have given architecture meaning. More precisely, everything that seems to have given architecture over to meaning. They deconstruct, first of all, but not only, the semantics of architecture.[16]

[16] Jacques Derrida, "Point de Folie – maintenant de l'architecture", translated by Kate Linker, in Neil Leach (ed.), *Rethinking Architecture*, Routledge, London, 1997, p 326.

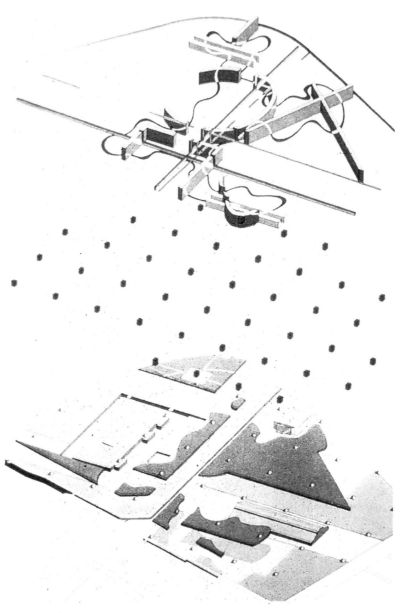

17 Bernard Tschumi, Parc de la Villette, Paris, 1985: Superimposition of lines, points and surfaces. (Bernard Tschumi)

As with Derrida's early preoccupation with language, there is an attempt to question deeply ingrained conventions, such that structures of meaning are not naturally "given" but are in fact historically "constructed". The metaphorical link with constructing makes architecture again an important theme – its persistence and all-pervasiveness makes it a significant target for reappraisal:

> This architecture of architecture has a history; it is historical through and through. Its heritage inaugurates the intimacy of our economy, the law of our hearth (*oikos*), our familial, religious and political *oikonomy*, all the places of birth and death, temple, school, stadium, agora, square, sepulchre. It goes right through us to the point that we forget its very historicity: we take it for nature. It is common sense itself.[17]

The shaking up of these common-sense assumptions about architecture's immovable orthodoxies is what Derrida discerns most clearly in the design of Tschumi's follies. He sees it as a creative process and a way of giving architecture another chance – against both the weight of inherited tradition and the modern conventions of economic and functional logic. In this he outlines a more positive approach to history, as an alternative to unthinking repetition:

> The *folies* affirm, and engage their affirmation beyond this ultimately annihilating, secretly nihilistic repetition of metaphysical architecture. They enter into the *maintenant* of which I speak; they maintain, renew and reinscribe architecture.[18]

Reaffirming the possibilities of architecture as a language of materiality and space has arisen from a process of questioning such modernist doctrines as "form follows function". The best examples of this process in action occur where the function itself is unclear, such as in the extension to the Jewish Historical Museum in Berlin, currently

---

[17] Jacques Derrida, "Point de Folie – maintenant de l'architecture", translated by Kate Linker, in Neil Leach (ed.), *Rethinking Architecture*, Routledge, London, 1997, p 326.
[18] Jacques Derrida, "Point de Folie – maintenant de l'architecture", translated by Kate Linker, in Neil Leach (ed.), *Rethinking Architecture*, Routledge, London, 1997, p 328.

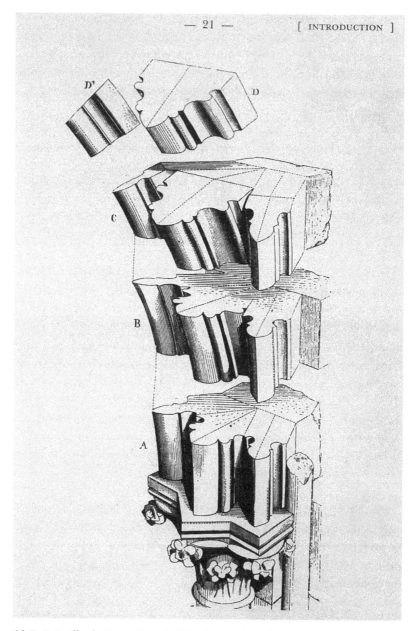

18 E. E. Voillet-le-Duc – Detail of Gothic vaulting from Dictionnaire
Raissonée, 1854–68

19 Zaha Hadid – Vitra Fire Station (model), Weil-am-Rhein, Germany, 1988–94. (Zaha Hadid)

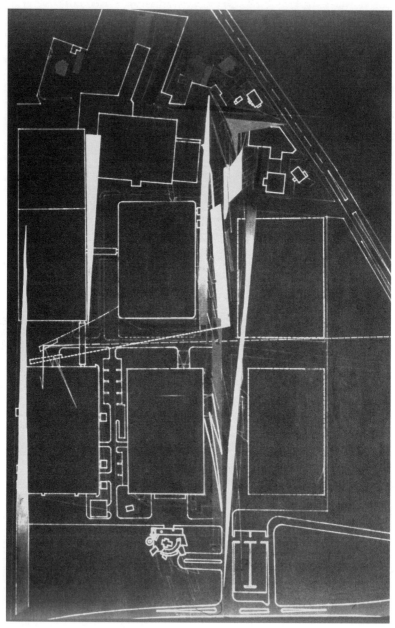

20 Zaha Hadid – Vitra Fire Station (painting), Weil-am-Rhein, Germany, 1988–94. (Zaha Hadid)

21 Zaha Hadid – Vitra Fire Station. (Christian Richters)

under construction. Daniel Libeskind has here designed a memorial, rather than a functioning museum in the traditional sense, and it is unclear whether the installation of exhibits will add to or detract from its effect. The powerful sense of loss and displacement which the building's empty spaces already invoke is a reminder that architecture's uniqueness can never be captured in a programme of requirements.

Another building which transcended its original function, in the attainment of a sculptural expression, was designed for the furniture company Vitra for its campus-like headquarters in Germany. The building by Zaha Hadid which was completed in 1994 began life as the site's private fire station but eventually became part of the company museum. The tension between rest and activity in the movements of the building's projected inhabitants produced a dynamic composition of

22 Zaha Hadid – Vitra Fire Station. (Christian Richters)

overlapping planes in an attempt to express the drama of its function. While this seems to have caused some problems for its originally intended users, it raises the whole question of the use of architecture as a means of functional or historical critique. A more explicit example of this kind of challenge to intended uses can be found in Peter Eisenman's early work in domestic architecture from the 1970s. The most famous of these is probably the House VI or Frank House, built in Connecticut in 1973 and much written about since. The house is an extreme example of architecture as an autonomous language, with its own system of compositional devices based on line, plane and volume. Like the architect's other designs of this period, the form is generated through a strategy of transformation, by subjecting an initially simple volume to a series of distortions, rotations and omissions. The most dramatic effect of this geometric discipline is the slot that appeared in the middle of the master bedroom, forcing the clients to sleep in sep-

23 Peter Eisenman – House Six, Axonometrics, 1976. (Peter Eisenman)

arate beds in order to preserve the formal integrity of the concept. This is obviously a somewhat indulgent piece of planning, which later fell victim to the owners' alterations, but the columns that occurred in the middle of the dining area also suggested new patterns of habitation. As Eisenman himself wrote, in *House of Cards*:

> The design process of this house, as with all the architectural work in this book, intended to move the act of architecture from its complacent relationship with the metaphysic of architecture, by reactivating its capacity to dislocate; thereby extending the search into the possibilities of occupiable form.[19]

This kind of questioning of the accumulated traditions enshrined in the institution of dwelling is a theme that the philosopher Andrew

[19] Peter Eisenman, *House of Cards*, Oxford University Press, New York, 1987, p 169.

Benjamin picks up on, in relation to deconstruction in philosophy. Rather than assume that this kind of criticism can only be carried out in conceptual terms, Eisenman's building actually "enacts" this process, according to Benjamin, in the very medium it is attempting to criticise. This deliberate blurring of disciplinary categories between the theory and practice of a "critical" architecture is something that Derrida has also set out to demonstrate, between philosophy and the language of literature. As Benjamin writes, describing the context in which this kind of building should be understood:

> Eisenman's work, the experience of that work, the philosophy demanded by it, opens up the need to think philosophically beyond the recuperative and nihilistic unfolding of tradition. Tradition is housed - since there is no pure beyond - but the housing of tradition takes place within a

24 Rem Koolhaas (Office for Metropolitan Architecture) – Kunsthal, Rotterdam, 1987–92. (Alistair Gardner)

25 Rem Koolhaas (Office for Metropolitan Architecture) – Kunsthal, Rotterdam, 1987–92. Interior showing columns in lecture hall. (Alistair Gardner)

plurality of possibilities that can no longer be foreclosed by function, by teleology or the aesthetics of form.[20]

This project is therefore a clear example of the notion touched on earlier, that architectural ideas exist at many different levels – in drawings, writings and models and not merely in completed buildings. The fact that some of these ideas have been obscured through the changes to the building during its life should not detract from the value of the project as a demonstration of architecture's "critical" capacities.

Rescuing the question of meaning from the reduction of architecture to engineering has been a preoccupation in architectural theory for at least the last several decades. It is this theme, which has only been touched on in this section, which will now become the central question in the remaining chapters. The following sections will map out the territory between the two positions discussed so far, which could be seen to mark the opposite poles of the argument over meaning and interpretation in architecture.

Suggestions for further reading

Background

Monroe Beardsley, *Aesthetics: From Classical Greece to the Present, A Short History*, Macmillan, New York, 1966.

John D. Caputo, *Deconstruction in a Nutshell: A Conversation with Jacques Derrida*, Fordham University Press, New York, 1997.

Jacques Derrida, "The End of the Book and the Beginning of Writing", in *Of Grammatology*, translated by Gayatri C. Spivak, Johns Hopkins University Press, Baltimore, 1976, pp 6–26.

Hans-Georg Gadamer, "The Relevance of the Beautiful" in *The Relevance of the Beautiful and Other Essays*, Robert Bernasconi (ed.), Cambridge University Press, Cambridge, 1986, pp 3–53.

---

[20] Andrew Benjamin, "Eisenman and the Housing of Tradition", in Neil Leach (ed.), *Rethinking Architecture*, Routledge, London, 1997, p 300.

Albert Hofstadter and Richard Kuhns, *Philosophies of Art and Beauty: Selected Readings in Aesthetics From Plato to Heidegger*, University of Chicago Press, Chicago, 1964.

Richard Kearney, "Jacques Derrida", in *Modern Movements in European Philosophy*, Manchester University Press, Manchester, 1986, pp 113-33.

Christopher Norris, *Deconstruction: Theory and Practice*, Routledge, London, 1991.

Foreground

Jacques Derrida, "Point de Folie – maintenant de l'architecture", translated by Kate Linker, in *AA Files*, No. 12/Summer 1986. Reprinted in Neil Leach (ed.), *Rethinking Architecture*, Routledge, London, 1997, pp 324-47.

Peter Eisenman, "Post-Functionalism", in Oppositions, 6/Fall 1976. Reprinted in K. Michael Hays (ed.), *Architecture Theory Since 1968*, MIT Press, Cambridge, MA, 1998, pp 236-9.

John Rajchman, *Constructions*, MIT Press, Cambridge, MA, 1998.

Bernard Tschumi, "Abstract Mediation and Strategy", in *Architecture and Disjunction*, MIT Press, Cambridge, MA, 1994, pp 190-206.

Mark Wigley, "The Translation of Architecture: The Production of Babel", in *Assemblage*, 8/1989. Reprinted in K. Michael Hays (ed.), *Architecture Theory Since 1968*, MIT Press, Cambridge, MA, 1998, pp 660-75.

Readings

Andrew Benjamin, "Eisenman and the Housing of Tradition", in *Architectural Design*, 1-2/1989. Reprinted in Neil Leach (ed.), *Rethinking Architecture*, Routledge, London, 1997, pp 286-301.

Robert Mugerauer, "Derrida and Beyond", in Kate Nesbitt (ed.), *Theorising a New Agenda for Architecture: An Anthology of Architectural Theory 1965-1995*, Princeton Architectural Press, New York, 1996.

Part 2

Models of Interpretation

3

The Return of the Body
Phenomenology in Architecture

In Chapters 1 and 2 the problematic status of architecture as a discipline was presented as an argument between what the writer C. P. Snow referred to as the "two cultures", of science and the arts.[1] Snow, in his Rede Lecture of 1959, was describing what he saw as a deep division in modern society, between those involved in quantitative work – such as scientific research and engineering – and those engaged in more qualitative fields, such as literature, music and fine art. The problem for Snow was the lack of communication between these two groups who seemed suspicious of each other's objectives, and in architecture, this situation has developed into an argument over the relevance of *meaning*. The two cultures within architecture embody a similar disagreement over the qualitative versus the quantitative approach to design. The historical material set out in the first two chapters of this book described the background to these two ways of thinking.

In reality, of course, architecture is inevitably caught in the middle between the "autonomous" realm of free artistic expression and the "deterministic" activity of applied engineering. As the German philosopher Theodor Adorno made clear, in an essay entitled "Functionalism

---

[1] C. P. Snow, *The Two Cultures and the Scientific Revolution*, Cambridge University Press, Cambridge, 1961.

Today", this split is actually brought about by a false opposition between purpose*ful* and purpose-*free* objects. He was writing in response to the call by Adolf Loos for an architecture that was free of "unnecessary" ornament, but this definition of what was necessary in the design of a building was seen by Adorno as fundamentally problematic. He described how the two issues were historically connected – such that ornament often derived from construction – and, by the same token, how supposedly "pure" technical objects soon acquired symbolic significance for their users. In the latter case this would apply to large scale structures, like the Eiffel Tower or the Brooklyn Bridge, and on a smaller scale this can also be seen in people's relationships with their cars or computers. The implications of Adorno's essay for this discussion concern the notion of architectural expression, the fact that even though one might attempt to design a purely functional building, one can't avoid the question of meaning. As soon as one produces something, of whatever description, one unavoidably enters the realm of representation. To use a linguistic analogy to express this idea more simply, one cannot separate what is said from the manner of the saying. If architecture, thus, is inevitably caught up in the complex web of cultural "languages", then questions of interpretation become more important, in order to understand the full potential of design.

Having established that architecture should be seen as a "language" of expression, as well as a means of providing useful enclosure, the final three chapters of this book set out possible strategies of interpretation, as a means to bridge the gap between the two cultures mentioned above. All three involve some compromise between the two tendencies described already, in terms of the "objectivity" of science versus the "subjectivity" of art, although in this chapter the debate leans somewhat towards the latter.

Phenomenology is a philosophy that considers the individual's experience – although with the ultimate aim of producing a solid basis for knowledge – and as such has proved particularly influential in architecture, due in large part to its emphasis on perception and cognition. The term itself has been the subject of considerable confusion, as different philosophers have made use of it in different ways, and although the dictionary definition adds some clarity to the issue it still leaves much room for debate. The word itself translates as the study of how phenomena appear to the consciousness, based on the Greek words *phaino* and *logos*. *Phaino* means "to show" or "come to appearance" and is also the root word of phantom and fantasy, while *logos* can mean "reason", "word" or "speak", hence its use in the sciences for "the study of".

The Meaning of "Being" – From Husserl to Heidegger

The current understanding of the term phenomenology comes from the German philosopher Edmund Husserl, who wrote in the early part of the twentieth century and who influenced much of the later work on the subject. Hegel, too, had used the term in his philosophy, as in the *Phenomenology of Spirit* already mentioned and in his case this also referred to a "coming to appearance" of things, in the sense that all objects were seen as manifestations of the creative force or spirit. Like Hegel, Husserl was also concerned with the search for certainty in our knowledge of the world, and both philosophers also referred back to the work of Kant. Kant had addressed this question of the relations between the mind and the world in his enquiries into the "conditions of possibility" of knowledge, but he had concluded that reality "in itself" was unknowable – that the mind was denied complete access to the outside world. In Kant's view the mind produces its own version of reality, one shaped by our cognitive capacities, although this can result in the conclusion that we see the world through a veil, or a distorting mirror which – inevitably, some would argue – obstructs our understanding. Later philosophers would interpret this in a more positive light but in Husserl's time this was seen as a shortcoming – the admission by philosophy that its ideas were unreliable and lacking the objective truth of modern science. The desire to raise philosophy to the level of a "rigorous science" inspired Husserl in his quest for a new approach: he was determined to find a way in to this realm of things-in-themselves, by examining the way things appeared to the mind.

In one sense this notion of a scientific philosophy could be seen as part of the continuing Enlightenment "project", with many disciplines including even the new social sciences still under pressure to fit the definitions of objectivity. The method that Husserl adopted for his study of phenomena and the ways that they present themselves to the mind were also reminiscent of Descartes' thought process, in his earlier search for the foundations of true knowledge. Like Descartes, Husserl began by abandoning all previous experience, regarding it as doubtful, uncertain or misleading and, having suspended his preconceptions he would "bracket off" a particular object, allowing him to contemplate it detached from its context. Having achieved this with the thing under study he then set about uncovering its essence. He did this by a process of "free variation" where an object's attributes are each considered in turn. By varying the characteristics an object possesses until it ceases to be the thing that it is, a core set of properties can eventually be identified which express the thing's underlying essence. One can try this with an everyday object like a table lamp and imagine substituting each of its features – one can change the flex or the shade without it ceasing to be a lamp, but removing the light source would transform it beyond recognition.

This is a crude example of what was a complex process for Husserl, referring to it as an *eidetic* reduction, from the Greek *eidos*, meaning ideal or essence, which Plato had also used in a similar sense. For Plato this referred to the unchanging idea or universal "type", of which any object was a particular example, and in Husserl's work this formed the first step of a larger process, which he referred to as the "phenomenological reduction". The initial element in this method is the bracketing off mentioned above, which leads to the isolation of the object from its context. By reducing the cultural world to the "life world", or the realm of immediate experience, Husserl hoped to achieve an unobstructed view of reality. The final movement in this sequence is the "transcendental reduction" which assumes that the experience of the individual can be applied universally. From the individual subject one is meant to extrapolate towards the universal realm of subjectivity in general – the unique experience of the particular individual is extended to apply to a "transcendental subject". All this was meant to provide the necessary scientific objectivity to the kind of philosophy which Husserl was developing, and it was suggested that this would achieve a certainty of knowledge that even the "normal" sciences could barely approach. As one commentator described it:

> . . . it appears that all non-philosophical sciences start from a complex of presuppositions which are not clarified in these sciences themselves. Philosophy, on the other hand, does not want to leave anything unsolved; it wants to reduce everything to primary 'presuppositions' which do not need to be clarified because they are immediately evident . . .[2]

Husserl's attempt to claw back the ground that had been lost to the physical sciences, in his claim to provide objective truths about the world, led him to an over-ambitious goal for his philosophy, which he admitted in his later work had failed to fully materialise. Even his famous slogan "back to the things themselves" had been somewhat belied by his emphasis on the study of universals. This abstraction in his approach cut him off from history and culture, and failed to capture the full depth of our experience of the world and, with his leaning towards a purely intellectual analysis, the role of the body in perception was played down. While in his later writings, particularly *The Crisis of the European Sciences*, he did suggest the importance of considering these wider themes, it was left to Husserl's students to develop them in detail, in ways that have since become significant in the course of recent philosophy.

Martin Heidegger was perhaps the most illustrious of those students. He came to study with Husserl at the University of Freiburg, and most of the leading figures in later Continental philosophy owe a great deal to his influence, whether direct or not. Although in Heidegger's later work he moved back to the study of language – as the ultimate source of knowledge or, as he described it, the "house of being" – it was in his early writings that he turned the phenomenological methods towards

---

[2] Joseph K. Kockelmans, *Phenomenology: The Philosophy of Edmund Husserl and its Interpretation*, Anchor Books, New York, 1967.

"lived" experience and away from Husserl's abstract "essences". The reason for this shift came from Heidegger's overall intention, to study the nature of *being*, not merely the nature of *knowing*. This distinction caused the argument between Heidegger and Cassirer on the status of art discussed in Chapter 2 and Heidegger felt Husserl had restricted his thinking, by considering epistemology at the expense of ontology. It was this larger preoccupation with the "meaning of being" that was to drive Heidegger's philosophy throughout his long and prolific career.

His approach to this question has also proved influential in architecture, as he set out to study the philosophical implications of the concrete experience of everyday reality. He followed Husserl's instruction to go "back to the things themselves", but this time as part of a larger historical context. Here emerges Heidegger's attempt at deconstruction, as we saw in Chapter 2, in terms of his "overcoming" of Western philosophy. He blamed that tradition for suppressing these difficult questions, partly by its insistence on the separation of the mind and the body – expressed in philosophical terms as the split between the subject and the object. This same split occurs in the debate between rationalism and empiricism – or between the reliability of data from the senses versus the "pure" concepts of the reasoning mind. This is the argument that phenomenology initially set out to transcend, by its concentration on the link between the two realms of the body and the mind. This overlap that occurs in the acts of perception and cognition was the underlying theme of Heidegger's study of the meaning of being – seen in terms of the German word *Dasein*, or "being-there". The first hints of phenomenology as a "philosophy of bodily experience" are contained in the first part of Heidegger's major book, *Being and Time* (1927). This book, which has since become a founding document for phenomenology, was published at the same time as he was editing another book with Husserl. The influence of his master's teaching is clear from his overall intentions, but his detailed concerns are directed more towards the description of everyday experience. The focus on "being-there" as the concrete counterpart to "being-as-such" was Heidegger's means of overcoming the abstractions of

Husserl's method. This principle that the study of existence must precede the understanding of essence is based on the notion that consciousness can only be understood as the consciousness *of* something. By studying the actual conditions of being-there, in a particular place at a particular time, Heidegger was able to suggest that there is no "essential" self prior to the *action* of the self in the world. It was this action that the self performs in its "reaching out" towards the world that became the key to resolving the subject–object split that had separated the mind from the body. This split which began with Plato and which was reinforced in the work of Descartes was now being addressed by phenomenology in terms of the relationship between interacting forces – the self is no longer a "disembodied mind" or just a fixed object amongst objects, but an ongoing "project" with a historical past and future possibilities.

This sense of temporality is what sets humans apart from other beings and likewise the responsibility of constructing the self as a project. This responsibility of the individual to carve out their own way in the world is a product of the idea of freedom, which formed the basis of "authentic" being. The freedom to set one's own objectives, according to a personal goal or project, carries with it what Heidegger claimed was an obligation to live up to being's "ownmost possibilities". The need to take responsibility for one's own destiny in the course of life became a defining characteristic of the existentialist branch of phenomenology – which was led by another of Husserl's students, the French philosopher Jean-Paul Sartre. What was significant about this emphasis on the theme of action in the world was the nature of the knowledge that was produced by the interaction between the body and its surroundings.

In an important passage of *Being and Time* Heidegger sets out a clear distinction between the two kinds of knowledge that emerge from the realms of action and contemplation. To illustrate this distinction he uses the famous example of a person with a hammer who, as they take up the tool and use it, gain access to an important mode of experience:

In dealings such as this, where something is put to use, our concern sub-ordinates itself to the 'in-order-to' which is constitutive for the equipment we are employing at the time; the less we just stare at the hammer-Thing, and the more we seize hold of it and use it, the more primordial does our relationship to it become . . . The hammering itself uncovers the specific 'manipulability' of the hammer. The kind of Being which equipment possesses – in which it manifests itself in its own right – we call 'readiness-to-hand'.[3]

The equipment, while in use, begins to "withdraw" from our per-ception, as we concern ourselves instead with the larger objective of the task itself. This will continue to be the case unless the tool breaks down in the course of its use, when it will suddenly step forward and assert itself again as an object in its own right. This is described by Heidegger as the condition of being "present-at-hand", and applies to all those objects that we can't make use of – like works of art or natu-ral phenomena. These objects which are not considered as equipment, in the sense of being tools or material resources, demand a contem-plative mode of understanding, as opposed to the active mode of use.

"Dwelling" and Building – Heidegger and Ortega

Another important notion for later writers on technology is the idea that a piece of equipment forms part of a network or pattern of related activities. A tool such as the hammer can only be meaningfully interpreted when it is seen in terms of the other tools involved in the performance of a particular function. The Spanish philosopher, José Ortega y Gasset, who also wrote on the philosophy of technology, coined the term "pragmatic fields" to explain this characteristic of items of equipment. The fact that all tools can be seen as belonging to particular activities means that to understand one item we must see it in context with a number of others. This is also extended

---

[3] Martin Heidegger, *Being and Time*, translated by John Macquarrie and Edward Robinson, Harper & Row, New York, 1962, p 98.

in Heidegger's writing into an architectural dimension, when he describes the understanding of a room as more than simply the space between four walls. As "equipment for residing" it implies a series of activities and related objects, such as the ink-stand, pen, paper, blotting pad, lamp, desk, chair and window that provide the example of the writer's study. These objects form an "arrangement" and provide a context for our understanding, where each item implies the others which are also necessary to the larger function of the room.

As a means of understanding buildings in terms of their activities, this logic is then extended into the natural domain, as Heidegger goes on to describe the ways in which equipment provides information about the outside world. A railway station with its covered platforms takes account of the local climate, and the use of street lighting tells us something about the variation in daylight through the year. Along with these environmental qualities there is the user, whose presence is also implied by the item of equipment, as the interpretation can be extended from the activity towards the person taking part in it.

While on one hand the above analysis sets the two kinds of knowledge – action and contemplation – in opposition to each other, Heidegger is also keen to establish the necessary interaction between these two ways of engaging with the world:

> 'Practical' behaviour is not 'atheoretical' in the sense of 'sightlessness'. The way it differs from theoretical behaviour does not lie simply in the fact that in theoretical behaviour one observes, while in practical behaviour one *acts*, and that action must employ theoretical cognition if it is not to remain blind; for the fact that observation is a kind of concern is just as primordial as the fact that action has *its own* kind of sight.[4]

This notion of an "embodied" knowledge which comes from engaging with the world of things forms the basis for contemplation in the projection of future possibilities for action. This emphasis on the interrelation between action and contemplation is what gives Heidegger's

---

[4] Martin Heidegger, *Being and Time*, translated by John Macquarrie and Edward Robinson, Harper & Row, New York, 1962, p 99.

early writing its existentialist orientation. This view, where the world is experienced *before* the mind describes it in concepts – where "existence precedes essence", according to the famous existentialist slogan – is contradicted to a certain extent by the direction of Heidegger's later thinking, when he moves back through a philosophy of language towards a more essentialist orientation.

What later writers called the *Kehre* or "turning" in Heidegger's work, occurs around the time of World War 2 during a difficult period in the philosopher's career. As Rector of Freiburg University in the period before the war, he failed to oppose the rise of National Socialism and this tarnished his reputation. In the late 1940s he was left without a formal teaching position, but he used this time to carry out further research and this deeply affected his later thinking. The shift in Heidegger's thought is the "turn" to language as a privileged realm, as we saw in his discussion of art and poetry, described in Chapter 2. More specifically, in terms of architecture, his interest was likewise centred on language, as he describes in the famous essay, "Building, Dwelling, Thinking". The order of priority suggested by the title – that one builds first, in order to dwell – is actually reversed in Heidegger's thinking, such that one must learn to dwell in order to build. This argument is based on the idea that we have "forgotten" what dwelling means, in the same way that Western philosophy has forgotten, or neglected, the true meaning of *Being*. In order to retrieve this original meaning Heidegger looks back into the history of language, to a time before Plato's troublesome division between the world of experience and the realm of ideal forms. In this pre-Socratic world, as it has since been referred to, Heidegger discerns a more authentic language, where a natural correspondence is supposed to have existed between ideas and words.

Through a series of etymologies based on the Greek and German languages, he uncovers a number of interrelations between the words connected with building and ideas about the meaning of being. In another essay from 1951, "Poetically Man Dwells", he gives a further account of the importance of the history that is "sedimented" within language:

But where do we humans get our information about the nature of dwelling and poetry? Where does man generally get the claim to arrive at the nature of something? Man can make such a claim only where he receives it. He receives it from the telling of language.[5]

He goes on to quote the line from Friedrich Holderlin's poem that gave the essay its title, which implies a certain "merit" in the physical acts of building. He compares this with the kind of construction involved in the cultivation of plants and the making of objects, but concludes that these are merely a consequence of the process of dwelling and not the "grounding" of dwelling itself. For this, man must look to poetry as the "authentic gauging of the dimension of dwelling"[6] which carries the history of dwelling within it, as well as the "projects" of future possibilities for building:

> Man is capable of such building only if he already builds in the sense of the poetic taking of measure. Authentic building occurs so far as there are poets, such poets as take the measure for architecture, the structure of dwelling.[7]

By way of a contribution towards this poetic background to the practice of architecture, Heidegger himself provided some intriguing insights in his earlier essay on the nature of dwelling. He describes the primordial character of human Being in terms of its location on the surface of the earth, which he develops into a notion called the "fourfold", which provides the background to the act of building. This four-way structure results from the way a building inhabits the interface of earth and sky – the implication of being *on* the earth is that of also being *under* the sky – while the second two terms cover divinities and mortals, which are more obscure and less clearly developed.

[5] Martin Heidegger, ". . . Poetically Man Dwells . . .", in *Poetry, Language, Thought*, translated by Albert Hofstadter, Harper & Row, New York, 1971, p 215. Reprinted in Neil Leach (ed.), *Rethinking Architecture*, Routledge, London, 1997.

[6] Martin Heidegger, ". . . Poetically Man Dwells . . .", in *Poetry, Language, Thought*, translated by Albert Hofstadter, Harper & Row, New York, 1971, p 227.

[7] Martin Heidegger, ". . . Poetically Man Dwells . . .", in *Poetry, Language, Thought*, translated by Albert Hofstadter, Harper & Row, New York, 1971, p 227.

While all four components are meant to be "presented", in the properly poetic activity of authentic dwelling, the discussion remains tantalisingly vague about the practical application of these ideas in architecure. Where Heidegger does become more specific is in his discussion of the definition of *place*, which he sees as the initial task involved in the acts of building and dwelling. On the one hand place is seen to be dependent on the articulation of boundaries and edge-conditions – the boundary is not where something stops, but where something actually "begins its presencing"[8] – and at the same time, places can be created through the intervention of a newly built object. He illustrates this with the example of the bridge, which brings the river banks into a new relationship, as it "causes" the banks to lie opposite to one another and "*gathers* the earth as landscape around the stream".[9]

These ideas begin to suggest a role for architecture, in heightening our awareness of the character of our surroundings, as did Heidegger's earlier analyses in the book *Being and Time*, where he considered the interpretation of items of equipment. In the end, however, language retains its status as the privileged medium or "house of being" and this view has caused much controversy ever since Heidegger first presented the essay "Building, Dwelling, Thinking" as a lecture. At the same conference, the Darmstadt Colloquium, which took place in August 1951, Ortega y Gasset presented his paper (mentioned above) on pragmatic fields. Their argument concerned the priority between action and contemplation, or between existence and essence in the understanding of the nature of dwelling. Ortega's "project of life" had become a "project of thought" in Heidegger's work, whereas the dialectical relationship between the two realms was still undeveloped in either version. It was left to other philosophers to return to this theme and to consider the specific role of bodily experience – to

---

[8] Martin Heidegger, "Building, Dwelling, Thinking", in *Poetry, Language, Thought*, translated by Albert Hofstadter, Harper & Row, New York, 1971, p 154. Reprinted in Neil Leach (ed.), *Rethinking Architecture*, Routledge, London, 1997.

[9] Martin Heidegger, "Building, Dwelling, Thinking", in *Poetry, Language, Thought*, translated by Albert Hofstadter, Harper & Row, New York, 1971, p 152.

escape what Michel Foucault would later call the "prison-house of language" – and provide a clearer understanding of the nature of "embodied" knowledge.

A Philosophy of the Body – From Bergson to Merleau-Ponty

Perhaps the most intriguing of those later writers who took up this theme of embodiment is the French philosopher Maurice Merleau-Ponty, who collaborated closely with Jean-Paul Sartre. The two men founded the philosophical journal *Les Temps Modernes* in 1945 and continued to work together on it until a disagreement forced them to part company. The same year that the journal was founded saw the publication of Merleau-Ponty's major work, the results of his doctoral research entitled *The Phenomenology of Perception*. In this work he first set out the effect that the body has on our perception, through a series of detailed analyses based on case studies from clinical research. By considering the way the senses work together in the process of *synaesthesia*, and how perception provides the raw data that the mind arranges into clear concepts, Merleau-Ponty hoped to show that language itself is merely derived from our lived experience and thereby to reverse the priority given to it in Heidegger's earlier analysis. As he describes it in the preface to his book:

> To return to the things themselves is to return to that world which precedes knowledge, of which knowledge always speaks, and in relation to which every scientific schematization is an abstract and derivative sign-language, as is geography in relation to the countryside in which we have learnt beforehand what a forest, a prairie or a river is.[10]

What Merleau-Ponty is trying to describe is a kind of pre-linguistic understanding, the notion that the world is already meaningful for us before it is "parcelled up" into language. His research led him, not

[10] Maurice Merleau-Ponty, *The Phenomenology of Perception*, translated by Colin Smith, Routledge, London, 1962, p ix.

surprisingly, away from the history of philosophy as such, to consider instead the role that *action* plays in our perception of the outside world. Although in this early work he had looked at spoken language in terms of its origins in the "language" of gesture – to claim that gesture was still an important factor in communication – he went on in his later essays to look at other means of expression, such as how an artist might use his body to communicate ideas in physical form. In the essay "Eye and Mind", published in 1961, Merleau-Ponty described the body as an interface between the perceiving mind and the physical world. His interest in the work of art came from its expression of this interaction, such as where the brush strokes in a painting reveal the movements of the artist's hand. This "encounter" between the artist's body and the natural resistance of the medium being used provides a powerful image of the everyday process of interaction between the body and the world. As another French philosopher, Henri Bergson, wrote in 1896: "The objects which surround my body reflect its possible action upon them."[11] Merleau-Ponty saw this reflection or revelation of the body's actions in the tectonic qualities of the work of art – this suggested the idea of continuity between the body and the outside world.

The American philosopher John Dewey, in the book *Art as Experience*, also used a similar formulation to explain his understanding of the work of art:

> The epidermis is only in the most superficial way an indication of where an organism ends and its environment begins. There are things inside the body that are foreign to it, and there are things outside of it that belong to it. . . .[12]

He suggested that as the biology of human life requires the taking in of air and foodstuffs, then one could also interpret the use of tools as a kind of "incorporation" of objects into the body. This discussion brings him close to the early Heidegger, in his analysis of the "ready-to-

[11] Henri Bergson, *Matter and Memory*, translated by N. M. Paul and W. S. Palmer, Zone Books, New York, 1988, p 21.
[12] John Dewey, *Art as Experience*, Perigee Books, New York, 1934, p 59.

hand", particularly the way the tool in use becomes "transparent" to the person using it. This idea of reaching out into the environment – in the sense of the tool as an extension of the body – becomes a major theme in Merleau-Ponty's work, particularly in his unfinished writings published just after his death. Earlier, in his book *The Phenomenology of Perception*, he had described a common scenario, where a person driving a new car takes a period of time to become accustomed to its size. With experience the person can feel whether the car will fit through a particular opening, as the volume of the vehicle becomes gradually incorporated into the overall "body image". Likewise in the case of a blind person who has to navigate with the aid of a stick, the tip becomes the point of sensitivity and a means of communication with the surrounding environment. The stick becomes a part of the body as the person eventually learns to feel things "through" it and, like Heidegger's hammer, it "withdraws" from our perception as the world is experienced at the tip of the cane.[13]

In his essay "The Intertwining - The Chiasm" which appeared in 1964, he developed the concept of the "flesh of the world" as a means of further exploring this idea. The intertwining referred to in the title is again that of the individual with the outside world, which he saw as a kind of transitional zone where the flesh of the body interacts with the "flesh" of things. Instead of a barrier between the mind and the world, he saw the body as our means of contact – the only means we have available for the task of reaching out to understand the world:

> It is that the thickness of flesh between the seer and the thing is (as) constitutive for the thing of its visibility as (it is) for the seer of his corporeity; it is not an obstacle between them, it is their means of communication. . . . The thickness of the body, far from rivalling that of the world, is on the contrary the sole means I have to go unto the heart of the things, by making myself a world and by making them flesh.[14]

[13] Maurice Merleau-Ponty, *The Phenomenology of Perception*, translated by Colin Smith, Routledge, London, 1962, p 143.
[14] Maurice Merleau-Ponty, "The Intertwining - The Chiasm" in *The Visible and the Invisible*, translated by Alphonso Lingis, Northwestern University Press, Evanston, IL, 1968, p 135.

This quest for the heart of things has been phenomenology's major objective, ever since Husserl first set out his method of achieving a definition of "ideal" essences. This highlights the persistent problem of conceiving the relationship between the mind and the world, just as Kant had discovered in the eighteenth century, in trying to resolve the argument between rationalism and empiricism. As Kant concluded, our human faculties impose a set of limits on our potential knowledge and in attempting to define these limits the search has since shifted to the experience of the individual "embodied" subject. The problem for phenomenology has been the extension of these individual insights, to apply to other individual subjects as part of an "inter-subjective" realm. Like Kant's definition of beauty as something experienced subjectively, there is still a huge leap of faith required to accept that judgements are agreed upon universally. This rift between the individual and the diverse experience of the larger society is a persistent problem in phenomenology which many critics have been quick to point out.

In architecture there lies the possibility that this problem might be alleviated through the study of phenomenology's insights as part of the wider cultural world. This hope that phenomenology offers possibilities for resisting the reductive ideology of modern science has been expressed by various writers as part of a general disillusionment with the state of architecture in the twentieth century. As the architectural historian Alberto Perez-Gomez pointed out, in the introduction to his important work on the "crisis" in modern architecture:

> The problem that determines most explicitly our crisis, therefore, is that the conceptual framework of the sciences is not compatible with reality. The atomic theory of the universe may be true but it hardly explains real issues of human behaviour. The fundamental axiom of the sciences since 1800 has been 'invariance', which rejects, or at least is unable to cope with, the richness and ambiguity of symbolic thought.[15]

---

[15] Alberto Perez-Gomez, *Architecture and the Crisis of Modern Science*, MIT Press, Cambridge, MA, 1983, p 6.

Towards an Architecture of the Body

One writer who provides a stepping-stone between the realms of philosophy and architecture also demonstrates the above dilemma in the development of his own career. The French phenomenologist Gaston Bachelard began as a philosopher of science, publishing a series of books on contemporary scientific issues during the 1920s and 1930s. In 1938 he published a book called *The Psychoanalysis of Fire*, which inaugurated a new direction in his work and puzzled most of his former readers. The reason for the consternation was Bachelard's apparent rejection of his own principles – instead of scientific methods of analysis, he now seemed to be more interested in poetry. In fact, Bachelard set out to answer the problem Perez-Gomez tried to answer (described above) that while science might provide precise definitions of things, these no longer seemed to mean anything in terms of our everyday experience. The notion that we understand things in terms of images, or by "telling stories" about the world, became the major theme of Bachelard's subsequent research, which crossed over effectively into literary criticism. This first work set out the literary sources for our understanding of the phenomenon of fire, particularly the symbolic significance of different uses of fire and the type of associations that went along with it. This book formed the first part of a whole series on a similar theme, where Bachelard considered each of the traditional four elements in turn and their potential to inspire imagination and reflection. With books on air and water and a further two on different aspects of the earth, he provided substantial evidence of the kind of knowledge that he felt science was leading us away from – the kind of knowledge still expressed in art, with its direct appeal to the imagination. It was the depth of meaning in the poetic image that held the key to Bachelard's interest, and he pursued this theme into the realm of architecture with his 1958 book *The Poetics of Space*.

This work develops a range of ideas based on the poetic qualities of intimate spaces, beginning with the house and its associated imagery as described in literary sources. In the early chapters the house is considered in its idealised form, as both a hermit's hut and an image of the cosmos, and this is later developed in a series of comparisons to other ideas of comfort and enclosure. Descriptions of animal dwellings such as shells and nests, along with items of furniture like chests and wardrobes, are all examined for their imaginative potential in express-ing the different qualities of the "ideal" home. The implication of Bachelard's examples, which are drawn in the main from poetry and fiction, is that a meaningful environment is one that will itself inspire a kind of poetic reverie. This activity of reflection by the solitary dreamer on the meaningful qualities of one's physical environment provides an interesting counterpart to Heidegger's notion that dwelling must always remain "worthy of questioning".[16] At the same time his collec-tion of resonant images could be seen as part of a design approach based on the memory of places. As the architect Peter Zumthor has written in a recent collection of essays:

> When I concentrate on a specific site or place for which I am going to design a building, if I try to plumb its depths, its form, its history, and its sensuous qualities, images of other places start to invade this process of precise observation: images of places that I know and that once impressed me, images of ordinary or special places that I carry with me as inner visions of specific moods and qualities; images of architectural situations, which emanate from the world of art, of films, theatre or literature.[17]

Bachelard's project of providing an "archive" for the activities of the "material imagination" provides a new way of understanding the kind of knowledge that architecture might express. As we no longer experience life in the abstract languages that have been produced by the physical sciences, we might consider Bachelard's use of the four elements as providing a phenomenological understanding of our envi-ronment. We can see how a work of architecture might contribute

---

[16] Martin Heidegger, "Building, Dwelling, Thinking", in *Poetry, Language, Thought*, translated by Albert Hofstadter, Harper & Row, New York, 1971, p 160.
[17] Peter Zumthor, *Thinking Architecture*, translated by Maureen Oberli-Turner, Lars Muller Publishers, Baden, 1998, p 36.

towards an awareness of these environmental qualities, if we consider a building like Fallingwater, the famous house by Frank Lloyd Wright. Completed in 1936 for the Pittsburgh retailer Edgar Kaufmann, the house was built as a weekend retreat, an escape from the pressures of city life. The site on Bear Run with its dramatic waterfall and rocky outcrops was well-known to the client's family from their summer weekends at a nearby cabin. They would often picnic along the river, around a campfire on the rock ledges, and it was this experience of the natural landscape that became the basis for Wright's design. The living room fireplace is built on an existing boulder, which is left as an "outcrop" rising up through the floor, and the spherical wine-kettle which is mounted above it also recalls the experience of outdoor cooking. The house itself provides an echo of the landscape, in its cantilevered ledges and continuous glazing – as though the terraces of the waterfall have been simply inhabited, like a series of cave-dwellings that might have existed already. This process of "concentration" of the site's existing characteristics is perhaps best evidenced in the way the building establishes different relationships with the water. From the entrance pool with its running fountain, to the open staircase suspended out over the river, the whole building provides an experience of water, even down to the stone flooring which recalls the river bed. This theme of the four elements creates a poetic image of the natural landscape, a kind of three-dimensional cosmic diagram in the sense that Bachelard would have appreciated. This building could also be read in terms of Heidegger's example of the way a bridge affects its surroundings, but for a direct application of these latter ideas we must look to other writers on architectural theory.

The Phenomenon of Place

In 1960 an early warning was sounded against the limitations of functionalism in architecture, in the manifesto written by two German architects and published in the Berlin journal *Der Monat*:

1 Frank Lloyd Wright – "Fallingwater", House for Edgar Kaufmann, Bear Run, Pennsylvania, 1935–39: Fireplace and wine kettle. (Jonathan Hale)

2 Frank Lloyd Wright – "Fallingwater", House for Edgar Kaufmann, Bear Run, Pennsylvania, 1935–39. (Jonathan Hale)

Architecture is a vital penetration of a multi-layered, mysterious, evolved and structured reality. Again and again it demands recognition of the *genius loci* out of which it grows. Architecture is no longer a two-dimensional impression but is becoming experience of corporeal and spatial reality, achieved by walking around and entering into . . . The subject–object relationship has been done away with . . . Architecture is the enveloping and sheltering of the individual, and hence a fulfilment and a deepening.[18]

This reintroduction of a phenomenological dimension into our interpretation of the built environment became significant in the reassessments of modernism that took place in the following decades.

[18] Reinhard Gieselmann & Oswald Mathias Ungers, "Towards a New Architecture", in Ulrich Conrads (ed.), *Programmes and Manifestoes on 20th Century Architecture*, Lund Humphries, London, 1970, p 166.

3 Frank Lloyd Wright – "Fallingwater", House for Edgar Kaufmann, Bear Run, Pennsylvania, 1935–39. (Jonathan Hale)

The Norwegian historian, Christian Norberg-Schulz, has been perhaps the most prolific of these recent writers, producing a series of
works that tries to question the dominant emphasis on functional
norms. He also utilised the concept of *genius loci* – spirit of the place
– in the book of the same name, subtitled "Towards a Phenomenology
of Architecture", and he also made use of many of the ideas we have
been discussing. Norberg-Schulz borrows directly from Heidegger's
work on the nature of dwelling, though he develops the ideas more
specifically through the notion of the "existential foothold":

> First of all I owe to Heidegger the concept of dwelling. 'Existential
> foothold' and 'dwelling' are synonyms, and dwelling, in an existential
> sense, is the purpose of architecture. Man dwells when he can orientate
> himself within and identify with, an environment, or, in short, when he
> experiences the environment as meaningful. Dwelling implies therefore
> something more than 'shelter'. It implies that the spaces where life
> occurs are places, in the true sense of the word.[19]

What gives a location its character, and transforms an abstract *space*
into a concrete *place*, is the way in which a work of architecture provides a visualisation of the *genius loci*. This can happen in various
ways, according to different cultures and historical traditions, and in
his earlier book *Meaning in Western Architecture* he set out to show
how this had occurred in the past. By analysing buildings of different
periods in terms of their common symbolic characteristics, he tried to
demonstrate how every culture has expressed its belief systems
through its architecture. Whether based on religious rituals or on the
structure of the cosmos, he tries to show how these narratives have
been "concretised", in ways specific to their geographical context.

In his later writings, these ideas were also applied to more recent
buildings, such as in the essay on Jorn Utzon concerning the theme
of earth and sky in his work. In Utzon's own essay "Platforms and
Plateaus", which looked at the landscape forms of sacred sites, he

[19] Christian Norberg-Schulz, *Genius Loci: Towards a Phenomenology of Architecture*,
Rizzoli, New York, 1980, p 5.

described the importance of the sculpted ground-plane, in the definition of a significant *place*. The dramatic juxtaposition with a hovering
roof-form, such as the outside of the Sydney Opera House and the inside
of the Bagsvaerd Church in Copenhagen, displays a similar Heideg-
gerian preoccupation with the building as an interface between earth
and sky. Norberg-Schulz also wrote on Louis Kahn, in another of his
later essays, discussing particularly his distinctive design approach
which is reminiscent of Husserl's bracketing. When beginning a project
for a school, Kahn tried to abandon his preconceptions and to rethink
the nature of the institution in terms of its essential characteristics:

> Schools began with a man under a tree who did not know he was a
> teacher, discussing his realisation with a few who did not know they
> were students. The students reflected on what was exchanged and how
> good it was to be in the presence of this man. They aspired that their sons
> also listened to such a man. Soon spaces were erected and the first
> schools became.[20]

Kahn thought of these "institutions" as the basic structures of
society and it was the task of a meaningful architecture to make them
visible to humanity. At the same time a building should make visible
the essential "structures" of the natural environment, particularly the
characteristics of the local landscape and the changing conditions of
natural light. The buildings for the Salk Institute in California and the
Kimbell Art Museum in Fort Worth both reveal these preoccupations
in their overall layout and choice of materials. The Salk provides a monumental plaza which opens the building up to view the wider landscape, and – as Heidegger would appreciate – to "receive" the sky. At
the Kimbell, Kahn's textured surfaces illustrate his idea of materiality
as "the giver of light", and also echo his famous saying that "the sun
never knew how great it was until it struck the side of a building".[21]

---

[20] Louis Kahn, quoted in Christian Norberg-Schulz, "The Message of Louis Kahn", in
Architecture: Meaning and Place, Selected Essays, Rizzoli, New York, 1988, p 201.
[21] Louis Kahn, quoted in Christian Norberg-Schulz, "The Message of Louis Kahn", in
Architecture: Meaning and Place, Selected Essays, Rizzoli, New York, 1988,
pp 203–5.

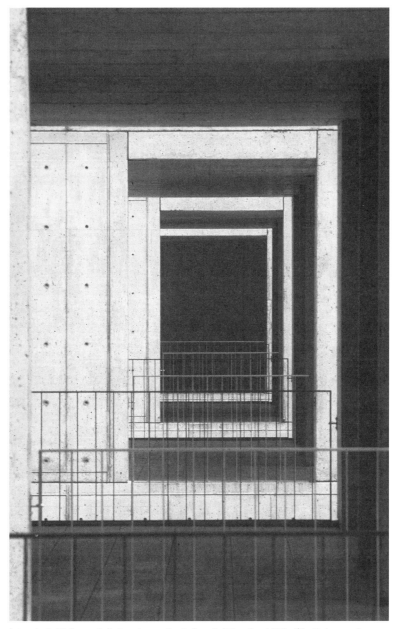

4 Louis I. Kahn – Salk Institute, La Jolla, California, 1959–65: Colonnade. (Neil Jackson)

5 Louis I. Kahn – Salk Institute, La Jolla, California, 1959–65: Plaza. (Neil Jackson)

6 Louis I. Kahn – Salk Institute, La Jolla, California, 1959–65: Plaza. (Neil Jackson)

7 Louis I. Kahn – Kimbell Art Museum, Fort Worth, Texas, 1966–72: Interior. (Jonathan Hale)

8 Louis I. Kahn – Kimbell Art Museum, Fort Worth, Texas, 1966–72. (Jonathan Hale)

9 Louis I. Kahn – Fisher House, Pennsylvania, 1960: Interior. (Jonathan Hale)

10 Louis I. Kahn – Fisher House, Pennsylvania, 1960. (Jonathan Hale)

On a smaller scale, this can also be seen in the design of the Fisher House in Pennsylvania, where the simple arrangement of timber boxes provides a dramatic "viewing-platform" over the landscaped site.

In the work of another writer, Kenneth Frampton, some of these ideas have been taken further, with the attempt to provide a programme for what he called a "critical regionalism". This would again address the idea of *place* but within the context of a "global" architecture, through a "critical" reinterpretation of vernacular building types and the use of local materials and craft skills. Frampton was again picking up on Heidegger and his attachment to the sense of place, though he identified a number of recent architects he felt had also been working on a similar theme. In the final chapter of his book *Modern Architecture: A Critical History*, he looked at the work of the Italian architect Carlo Scarpa, both as an example of a regional architecture and a seductive collage of sensuous materials. Frampton has since developed a more specific interest in tectonic culture in modern architecture and in a recent book he reinterpreted a number of key buildings in terms of their construction. This shift of interest towards architectural detail shows a further influence of phenomenological thinking, as the expressive potential of a building's materiality is seen as enriching the experience of form and space. As Marco Frascari – a former assistant of Scarpa's – wrote on this theme:

> In architecture feeling a handrail, walking up steps or between walls, turning a corner and noting the sitting of a beam in a wall, are coordinated elements of visual and tactile sensations. The location of those details gives birth to the conventions that tie a meaning to a perception.[22]

These two themes of place and bodily experience become for Frampton a mode of "resistance" – a way of countering the alienation of the city and the emphasis in our media culture on the sense of vision:

[22] Marco Frascari, "The Tell-the-Tale Detail", *VIA*, No. 7, 1984, p 28. Reprinted in Kate Nesbitt (ed.), *Theorising a New Agenda for Architecture: An Anthology of Architectural Theory 1965-1995*, Princeton Architectural Press, New York, 1996, p 506.

11 Carlo Scarpa – Architectural Institute of the University of Venice, Venice, 1966: Entrance. (David Short)

12 Carlo Scarpa – Querini Stampalia Foundation, Venice, 1961–63: Detail of bridge. (David Short)

Two independent channels of resistance proffer themselves against the ubiquity of the Megalopolis and the exclusivity of sight. They presuppose a mediation of the mind/body split in Western thought. They may be regarded as archaic agents with which to counter the potential universality of rootless civilisation. The first of these is the tactile resilience of the place-form; the second is the sensorium of the body. These two are posited here as interdependent, because each is contingent on the other. The place-form is inaccessible to sight alone just as simulacra exclude the tactile capacity of the body.[23]

While the preoccupation with the body has become a progressive theme in recent architecture, in Frampton's work it remains tied to a somewhat reactionary urban agenda – slightly too reminiscent of Heidegger's nostalgic longing for the "rooted" vernacular lifestyle of the pre-industrial Black Forest.

The Body in Space – Movement and Experience

Other architects who have worked on this theme of the perceiving body in its relation to space have begun to break away from the restrictive archetypes suggested by Frampton's critical regionalism. Among these might be counted Tadao Ando in Japan, Herzog and De Meuron in Europe and Steven Holl in America. With each of these architects, as in Louis Kahn's work, there is a desire to articulate material qualities, in order to heighten our perceptual awareness of the encounter between the body and the world of things. In Holl's own recent book *Intertwining*, he specifically engaged with the work of Merleau-Ponty and even used the term "Kiasma" to label his project for the Helsinki Art Museum. Among younger architects, Ben van Berkel has also been exploring this theme of movement, particularly in the Mobius House, recently completed. The design is based on interlocking use-patterns and the sequence of possible movements throughout the day and it

[23] Kenneth Frampton, "Intimations of Tactility: Excerpts from a Fragmentary Polemic", in Scott Marble *et al.* (eds), *Architecture and Body*, Rizzoli, New York, 1988.

was recently published along with two sets of photographs, one of the building and the other showing figures in motion. Reminiscent of fashion photography, this was the architect's decision, to try to capture the sub-conscious context behind the conceptual process:

> They are meant to be shown next to each other to express the two aspects mentioned above: the idea of movement as a structuring principle, and the way in which the specific architectural imagination is engaging with the collective imagination.[24]

On another level phenomenology has been used in various projects of "resistance", where the emphasis on bodily experience has exposed the limits of functional principles. This has also shown how deconstruction has been deeply influenced by phenomenology, particularly in Jacques Derrida's critique of Heidegger and its architectural counterpart in recent buildings. In this regard the writings of Bernard Tschumi could also be seen as part of this movement, particularly his early essays on the "Pleasure of Architecture" and the "erotic" dimension of spatial experience:

> Exceeding functionalist dogmas, semiotic systems, historical precedents, or formalised products of past social or economic constraints is not necessarily a matter of subversion but a matter of preserving the erotic capacity of architecture by disrupting the form that most conservative societies expect of it.[25]

Tschumi went on to develop this notion towards a new way of thinking about the use of space – his idea was to avoid the kind of functional specificity which he felt was stifling the real life of architecture. To this end he came up with the intriguing concept of the architecture of the "event":

---

[24] Ben van Berkel, "A Day in the Life: Mobius House by UN Studio/van Berkel & Bos", *Building Design*, Issue 1385, 1999, p 15.
[25] Bernard Tschumi, *Architecture and Disjunction*, MIT Press, Cambridge, MA, 1996, p 92.

13 Tadao Ando – Meditation Space, UNESCO, Paris, 1994–95.
(Jonathan Hale)

The very heterogeneity of the definition of architecture – space, action, and movement – makes it into that event, that place of shock, or that place of the invention of ourselves.[26]

This notion of self invention recalls the thinking of Merleau-Ponty on the work of art, particularly as a means of portraying the encounter between the artist and the things of the world. Tschumi also makes an interesting counterpoint to the idea of place as something fixed and stable, as he describes a more dynamic and flexible situation where activities themselves establish new kinds of places. This recalls Heidegger's notion of dwelling as an activity, something that must be constantly striven for and not something achieved or given, and at the same time it suggests a looser fit between a building's form and its functional programme. The follies at La Villette, for instance, illustrate this openness to future possibilities, being a series of initially unprogrammed spaces that different events might transform into places. The networks of paths and walkways at La Villette also highlight the importance of movement, suggesting a choreography of routes that recall Le Corbusier's "architectural promenade" – as seen at the Villa Savoye and the later Carpenter Centre.

The several problems with the influence of phenomenology in architecture tend to derive from the difficulties with the philosophy itself, not least of which is the emphasis on subjective experience and the problem of applying this kind of knowledge in a wider, social context. While it can certainly be productive as part of a detailed design process, particularly for the qualitative and sensory aspects of the experience of space, it can also prove useful as part of a more "critical" strategy, as the recent work in deconstruction has begun to suggest. Part of this relevance depends on our next topic, the other major source for the philosophy of deconstruction, based as it is on a critique of structuralism as a supposedly more objective approach to interpretation. In the conclusion we will look at other thinkers who have taken up the themes of phenomenology, but who have tried to consider

[26] Bernard Tschumi, *Architecture and Disjunction*, MIT Press, Cambridge, MA, 1996, p 258.

14 Le Corbusier – Carpenter Centre, Harvard University, Cambridge, MA, 1959–63. (Alistair Gardner)

15 Le Corbusier – Carpenter Centre, Harvard University, Cambridge, MA, 1959–63. (Alistair Gardner)

16 Le Corbusier – Carpenter Centre, Harvard University, Cambridge, MA, 1959–63. (Alistair Gardner)

them in terms of the wider issues, such as cultural contexts and historical traditions.

Suggestions for further reading

Background

Hubert L. Dreyfus, *Being-in-the-World: A Commentary on Heidegger's Being and Time, Division I,* MIT Press, Cambridge, MA, 1991.

Terry Eagleton, "Phenomenology, Hermeneutics, Reception Theory", in *Literary Theory: An Introduction*, University of Minnesota Press, Minneapolis, 1983, pp 54–90.

Richard Kearney, "Edmund Husserl", "Martin Heidegger" and "Maurice Merleau-Ponty", in *Modern Movements in European Philosophy*, Manchester University Press, Manchester, 1986.

Maurice Merleau-Ponty, "Preface" to *Phenomenology of Perception*, translated by Colin Smith, Routledge, London, 1962, pp vii–xxi.

George Steiner, *Martin Heidegger*, University of Chicago Press, Chicago, 1991.

Foreground

Gaston Bachelard, *The Poetics of Space*, translated by Maria Jolas, Beacon Press, Boston, 1969.

John Dewey, *Art as Experience*, Perigee Books, New York, 1980.

Kenneth Frampton, "Prospects for a Critical Regionalism", in *Perspecta*, 20/1983, reprinted in Kate Nesbitt (ed.), *Theorising a New Agenda for Architecture: An Anthology of Architectural Theory 1965–1995*, Princeton Architectural Press, New York, 1996, pp 470–82.

Steven Holl, *Intertwining*, Princeton Architectural Press, New York, 1996.

Christian Norberg-Schulz, "The Phenomenon of Place", reprinted in Kate Nesbitt (ed.), *Theorising a New Agenda for Architecture: An Anthology of Architectural Theory 1965–1995*, Princeton Architectural Press, New York, 1996, pp 414–28.

Alberto Perez-Gomez, "The Renovation of the Body", in *AA Files*, No. 13/Autumn 1986, pp 26-9.

Readings

Kenneth Frampton, "Rappel à l'Ordre: The Case for the Tectonic", in Architectural Design, 3-4/1990. Reprinted in Kate Nesbitt (ed.), *Theorising a New Agenda for Architecture: An Anthology of Architectural Theory 1965-1995*, Princeton Architectural Press, New York, 1996, pp 518-28.

Martin Heidegger, "Building, Dwelling, Thinking", in *Poetry, Language, Thought*, translated by Albert Hofstadter, Harper and Row, New York, 1971. Reprinted in Neil Leach (ed.), *Rethinking Architecture*, Routledge, London, 1997, pp 100-9.

Bernard Tschumi, "The Architectural Paradox", in *Architecture and Disjunction*, MIT Press, Cambridge, MA, 1994. Reprinted in K. Michael Hays (ed.), *Architecture Theory Since 1968*, MIT Press, Cambridge, MA, 1998, pp 218-28.

4

Systems of Communication
Structuralism and Semiotics

Phenomenology was introduced in Chapter 3 as emerging from Edmund Husserl's dream of philosophy as a legitimate and "rigorous" science. In order to place philosophy on a firm foundation of scientific certainty, he had attempted a return to the study of "things in themselves". This had led some philosophers to focus on the individual's subjective experience and the influence that the body has on our understanding of the world around us. As a consequence of this, phenomenology has been charged with being too restricted in its interest, considering things as isolated objects cut off from the social context of reality. On the other hand a more deterministic version has developed which sees language as the source of all meaning – affecting our understanding by limiting the way we think. In more recent years this emphasis on language has proved attractive in the shift towards science, as linguistics has developed a series of far-reaching interpretive models which have since been applied more generally to the understanding of culture as a whole. The innovations that inspired this dramatic transition are still central to our understanding of architecture today, as modernism, post-modernism and even deconstruction have all been affected by this new conception of language.

The discussion in Chapter 3 of the significance of places was intended to establish the importance of meaning in architecture. The fact that buildings, in a sense, can be "read" as cultural "texts" will now be the dominant theme of this and subsequent chapters. Where Chapter 3 looked at the issue of *what* buildings mean, in terms of the existential predicament of humanity and the search for a sense of belonging, this chapter considers the question of *how* buildings mean, using the philosophy of language that has become known as structuralism.

Our discussion of language so far in this book has centred on the issue of free will and determinism – the question of whether, as Heidegger suggested, it is man or language that speaks. Is man in fact the master of language or is language the master of man?[1] The idea that we are somehow restricted by language to repeating the meanings that have been established before us is suggested by Heidegger's etymological analyses that attempt to uncover so-called original meanings. This approach to the study of language as a continually developing historical phenomenon seems to ignore the way that the use of language alters meanings over time. The slightly arbitrary points in history that Heidegger chooses to look back to still suggest a rather unscientific understanding of the workings of language as a system. It was the problem of untangling these historically dependent issues that structuralism initially attempted to answer and in the process it created a much more systematic and scientific approach to language, which has since become a "science" of human culture. As critic Terry Eagleton has succinctly pointed out:

> Structuralism in general is an attempt to apply this linguistic theory to objects and activities other than language itself. You can view a myth, a wrestling match, system of tribal kinship, restaurant menu or oil painting as a system of signs, and a structuralist analysis will try to isolate the underlying set of laws by which these signs are combined into meanings. It will largely ignore what the signs actually 'say', and concentrate instead on their internal relations to one another. Structuralism, as Fredric Jameson has put it, is an attempt to rethink everything through once again in terms of linguistics.[2]

[1] Martin Heidegger, ". . . Poetically Man Dwells . . .", in *Poetry, Language, Thought,* translated by Albert Hofstadter, Harper & Row, New York, 1971, p 215. Reprinted in Neil Leach (ed.), *Rethinking Architecture,* Routledge, London, 1997.
[2] Terry Eagleton, *Literary Theory: An Introduction,* University of Minnesota Press, Minneapolis, 1983, p 97.

The reason for this turn towards language again – although in a way quite distinct from the turn in phenomenology – is the attempt to understand our relationship to the world in terms of the metaphors that we use to describe it. To get beyond the abstractions of science, as Gaston Bachelard tried to do, structuralism focused instead on the cognitive value of narratives, as a way of dealing with the fact that in everyday human terms, the universe is not made of atoms, it is "made of stories".[3]

The "Deep Structures" of Language – Ferdinand De Saussure

So what is this linguistic model that has proved so useful in so many disciplines and how does it differ from the treatment of language in the other philosophies considered so far? The model originates in the work of the Swiss linguist Ferdinand de Saussure and is described in his *Course in General Linguistics* which was assembled from notes and published as a book after his death in 1916. The three key principles of Saussure's analysis of language all follow from his initial observations on the nature of the "linguistic sign". The sign in language is the word or sentence, which operates by referring to the idea of an object in the mind, and can therefore be split into its two components – the *signifier*, or the word, and the *signified*, the idea of the object. Having devised this two-part structure he then developed the first of his controversial principles by insisting on the *arbitrary* nature of the connection between the two halves of the sign. Traditional linguistic studies had assumed a natural bond between sound and thing, such as in onomatopoeic words like "cuckoo", "drip" or "splash". By contrast, Saussure maintained that these formed only a small component of a language while the majority of the words we use were simply assigned to things by convention. As he writes in Part One of his *Course*:

---

[3] Muriel Rukeyser, quoted in Charles Moore, *Water and Architecture*, H. N. Abrams, New York, 1994, p 15.

Words like the French *fouet* 'whip' or *glas* 'knell' may strike certain ears with suggestive sonority, but to see that they have not always had this property we need only examine their Latin forms (*fouet* is derived from *fagus*, 'beech tree'; *glas* from *classicum*, 'sound of a trumpet'). The quality of their present sounds, or rather the quality that is attributed to them is a fortuitous result of phonetic evolution.[4]

This led Saussure to the observation that language operated as a "system of differences", where the functioning of words depended on their relationships with one another, rather than any necessary connection to the objects to which they refer. For example, there is nothing particularly animal-like about the words "rat" or "cat", whereas the difference between rat and cat is obviously quite significant to the meaning of a sentence. Communication is possible within this system due to the mutual agreement which governs its use, and this also depends on the user's knowledge of the conventions, without which the letters r-a-t would simply be three black marks on a page. This principle frees Saussure to concentrate on the *syntactic* dimension of language, the internal rules of combination which structure its operation, as opposed to the *semantic* dimension or the external reference and meaning. In other words, what Saussure is studying is the *form* rather than the *content* of language, isolating what for him is the most important aspect of the problem.

The second of Saussure's three principles emerged from this notion of language as a system, and concerned the distinction between the system in general and particular uses of it in the act of speaking. For this he made use of another binary opposition, described by the French terms *langue* and *parole*, which are usually left untranslated, to avoid the ambiguities of their English equivalents. *Langue* refers to language as a system, with its underlying structure of rules and conventions, which are then deployed like pieces in a chess game, in the process of communicating a particular meaning. These specific acts of *parole*, or "speech", are to some extent restricted by the potential of

---

[4] Ferdinand de Saussure, *Course in General Linguistics*, translated by Wade Baskin, McGraw-Hill, New York, 1966, p 69.

the system and it is this limitation of the individual's free expression that has proved the most controversial of Saussure's ideas. As the philosopher Richard Kearney has succintly pointed out:

> It implied a fundamental rejection of the romantic and existentialist doctrines that the individual consciousness or 'genius' is the privileged locus of the creation of meaning. In answer to Sartre's view, for example, that each individual existence is what each individual makes of it, the structuralist replies that the meaning of each person's *parole* is governed by the collective pre-personal system of *langue*.[5]

Saussure's third important principle is founded on a further binary opposition, this time concerned with the question of history and its relevance to the underlying structure of language. As Saussure had dismissed the notion of meaning as a product of the relationships between words and things, he was thereby also able to dispense with the ways these might have changed with the passage of time. He thus made the distinction between the *diachronic* study of language, which looks at its development across historical time, and his preferred *synchronic* analysis which isolates the system at a particular moment in a "frozen" state. It is here that Saussure departs most dramatically from the traditional habits of linguistic study, with its usual emphasis on philology and etymology and the complex interactions of cultural forces. Saussure concluded that while particular acts of *parole* may be continually changing with the passage of time, beneath these "surface" effects lay the deep and timeless structure of *langue*. At any point in history this deep structure could be subjected to analysis and this would always yield the most informative picture of the systems of meaning at work in language.

What Saussure laid out was a method of analysis which those who followed him applied in practice – he did not himself live long enough to develop the science of signs which he had already dreamt of and christened semiology:

---

[5] Richard Kearney, *Modern Movements in European Philosophy*, Manchester University Press, Manchester, 1986, p 245.

A science that studies the life of signs within society is conceivable; it would be a part of social psychology and consequently of general psychology; I shall call it *semiology* (from Greek *semeion* 'a sign'). Semiology would show what constitutes signs, what laws govern them. Since the science does not yet exist, no one can say what it would be . . . Linguistics is only a part of the general science of semiology; the laws discovered by semiology will be applicable to linguistics, and the latter will circumscribe a well-defined area within the mass of anthropological facts.[6]

Structures of Society – From Lévi-Strauss to Barthes

Appropriately, the first to occupy the territory staked out in Saussure's work was the French anthropologist Claude Lévi-Strauss, born in 1908, who is perhaps today the most closely associated with the spread of structuralism in cultural analysis. Lévi-Strauss had travelled in South America while teaching in Brazil in the 1930s, and based much of his later writing on this early experience working in the field. In one of his early works, *Tristes Tropiques*, published in 1955, he described his three major influences as "geology, Marxism and psychoanalysis" – he claimed that all three disciplines demonstrate that "the true reality is never the most obvious".[7] The principle in all these practices, that surface effects are invisibly determined by the influence of underlying structures, is an important factor in Chapter 5 of this book. For now, it is the language model that provided the structure for Lévi-Strauss' work, as he searched for a similar system of "differences" to that which Saussure had uncovered in language. As an anthropologist he studied societies that had changed very little with the passage of time and this allowed him to isolate them "synchronically", as Saussure had recommended with language.

---

[6]   Ferdinand de Saussure, *Course in General Linguistics*, translated by Wade Baskin, McGraw-Hill, New York, 1966, p 16.
[7]   Claude Lévi-Strauss, *Tristes Tropiques*, translated by John and Doreen Weightman, Penguin Books, New York, 1992, p 57.

In *The Elementary Structures of Kinship*, which first appeared in 1949, he applied this model to the laws governing marriage in various so-called primitive cultures. At first sight this application might seem somewhat inappropriate, as the make-up of family units appears to be not primarily a means of expression. Lévi-Strauss, however, demonstrates that these relationships are governed by laws – a complex network of codes and prohibitions that provides a sense of order and structure within a community. By this means, he shows that kinship laws act as a form of "representation", a symbolic language through which a community describes itself in structural terms. By following the authority of these implicit codes, a tribal grouping can maintain its sense of order, as individual decisions and actions can always be related to the larger patterns. Rather than the object-centred approach of traditional anthropology, which concentrated on the nuclear family unit as a basic building block of a society, Lévi-Strauss instead followed Saussure and considered the *relations between* these units. He observed that patterns of intermarriage followed a ritualised process of exchange, resulting in important bonds between groups of families, due to connections such as parents/siblings, children/cousins, etc. beyond the immediate child/parent relationship. The females were often "exchanged" in marriage, as part of this process of maintaining order, and a similar system often operated in other ritualised customs such as gift-giving, trading and religious practice. To Lévi-Strauss these patterns also betrayed the attempt to explain the underlying structures of nature, such as where the community forms a microcosm of the world, and *pro*creation becomes a metaphor for creation.

This is explained more comprehensively in what is probably Lévi-Strauss' most representative book, his collection of essays entitled *Structural Anthropology*, published in French in 1958. In this book he develops much further the analysis of cultural practices as forms of expression, with studies on the structural analysis of myth, alongside magic, religion and art. This work forms a parallel to his study of kinship in its emphasis on underlying order, in particular the idea that meaning emerges from the way basic units are combined into systems. Where Saussure had analysed language in terms of "phonemes", or units of sound, Lévi-Strauss identified "myth*emes*" as the units of meaning within a story. As with language, it was not the semantic reference of the individual mytheme that was most important: as he admitted, many myths contained quite superficial literal meanings. What was significant was the way in which the units were combined into a story, the presence or absence of particular characters and the sequence of events in which they were involved. Lévi-Strauss provided a demonstration of his theory in his analysis of the Oedipus myth, which he showed depended on a series of themes which are acted out by the figures in the story. He highlighted a series of general contradictions with which he claimed the myth was attempting to deal, such as the oppositions between culture and nature, male and female, marital relations and blood relations, together with the general mysteries of life and death and the origins of mankind. The fact that myths always address these fundamental dilemmas provides the true meaning beneath their surface appearance and they are thus composed, like works of art, to make sense out of the chaos of the world. This theme of imposing patterns upon the flux of everyday experience forms a parallel to techniques of psychoanalysis such as the interpretation or decoding of dreams.

The latter field uses the technique as a way of resolving psychological dilemmas and in a similar sense Lévi-Strauss sees a myth as a kind of interpretive or mediating device – an attempt to resolve the kind of oppositions set out in the list above. This theme is often taken up by a particular character within the story, such as with the trickster figure he discovered in the mythologies of the North American Indians. The trickster is a hybrid of mortal and divine being who appears in a range of different guises and is used to help make sense of mysterious phenomena by shifting from one mode of existence to another. This theme of the intermediary as a useful explanatory device also occurs in religious traditions in a somewhat similar role – the Greek gods who could adopt various human forms to interfere with everyday events and the figures of Christ and the angels as divine messengers of the word of God all have the ability to move between one world and another and are thereby used to explain away apparently contradictory aspects of experience.

These archetypal themes are played out in countless individual myths and Lévi-Strauss' ambitious intention was to provide a universal "template" for their interpretation. It is this emphasis on universality and the use of binary oppositions as units of meaning that lends his method its immediate impact as well as exposing its obvious limitations. The archetypal themes which appear in myths and seem to limit their potential meaning relate to the inherited structure of language that apparently limits the possibilities of expression. This "displacement" of the individual subject from its sovereign position as a free-thinking person is one effect of the structuralist view of the world which later philosophers attempted to address. The implicit determinism in Lévi-Strauss' approach to culture seems to result from his overreaction to phenomenology and existentialism – he disparaged their emphasis on the individual subject's experience and sought instead for a more objective means of analysing and interpreting reality. His quest, like Edmund Husserl's, for a truly "rigorous science", had resulted in a similarly isolated study of the "essential" structures of meaning.

Projecting some of these insights back into the social context of experience has been the task of those more recent writers who have been influenced by structuralist thinking. Of these, one of the most provocative is the French critic Roland Barthes, who also demonstrated in his later work the influence of structuralism on deconstruction. As Lévi-Strauss had already demonstrated that the linguistic model could be applied to social practices – such as marriage laws, religious rites, food preparation and so on – Barthes was able to extend this thinking into the context of contemporary culture and at the same time assess its political implications for our understanding of sign systems. Barthes also amplified Lévi-Strauss' analysis of the ways in which signs transmitted their meanings, based on two alternative ways of interpreting a word, either by category or position within a sentence. By this he meant that words could be understood as part of a continuous chain or sequence, where they acquire meaning by their position and context, and through their relationship with other words in the same sentence. On the other hand, they can be understood in terms of categories or groups of words, or as alternative nouns, verbs or adjectives chosen from those available within the system. This technique of interpretation can be seen more easily with a restaurant menu, where items can either be read as components of a meal, or simply as alternative starters, main courses or desserts. Table 1 shows Barthes' formalised version of this analysis, comparing a range of signifying practices and contrasting the "syntagmatic" (or sequential)

	System	Syntagm
Garment system	Set of pieces, parts or details which cannot be worn at the same time on the same part of the body, and whose variation corresponds to a change in the meaning of the clothing: tocque, bonnet, hood, etc.	Juxtaposition in the same type of dress of different elements: skirt, blouse, jacket.
Food system	Set of foodstuffs which have affinities or differences, within which one chooses a dish in view of a certain meaning: the types of entrée, roast or sweet.	Real sequence of dishes chosen during a meal: this is the menu.
	A restaurant menu actualises both planes: the horizontal reading of the entrées, for instance, corresponds to the system; the vertical reading of the menu corresponds to the syntagm.	
Furniture system	Set of the "stylistic" varieties of a single piece of furniture (e.g. a bed)	Juxtaposition of the different pieces of furniture in the same space: bed, wardrobe, table, etc.
Architecture system	Variations in style of a single element in a building, various types of roof, balcony, hall, etc.	Sequence of the details at the level of the whole building.

Table 1: "Syntagm and System", after Roland Barthes, *Elements of Semiology*, p. 63.

reading with the alternative "systematic" (or categorial) approach.[8] The gridded structure that Barthes makes use of here was often adopted by Lévi-Strauss, particularly for the complex analysis of mythemes in his later work on the science, or "logics", of myth.

Barthes, however, by contrast with Lévi-Strauss, used the term "myth" to refer to "ideology" which he saw as a way of distorting meaning in favour of a dominant political or economic power. The thinking behind this process of distortion will be dealt with more fully in Chapter 5, but for now it is important to recognise that Barthes also had another agenda – questioning the deterministic principle of Lévi-Strauss' linguistic model. Barthes does this by returning to the nature of the sign and the arbitrary attachment between signifier and signified, thereby challenging the inference in Lévi-Strauss' work that culture should be seen as a "static" system. If signs are agreed on by convention then Barthes claims they must be capable of change, and therefore to neglect the historical dimension of language leads to the confusion of nature and culture. As he wrote in his collection of essays, *Mythologies* (1957):

> The starting point of these reflections was usually a feeling of impatience at the sight of the 'naturalness' with which newspapers, art and common-sense constantly dress up a reality which, even though it is the one we live in, is undoubtedly determined by history . . . I resented seeing Nature and History confused at every turn, and I wanted to track down, in the decorative display of *what-goes-without-saying*, the ideological abuse which, in my view, is hidden there.[9]

Reflecting on matters as divergent as a wrestling match, *Elle* magazine, a plastics exhibition and the new Citroën DS, Barthes was constantly on the lookout for the political undercurrents in everyday experience. On the principle that every object is a sign and that every

[8]   Roland Barthes, *Elements of Semiology*, translated by Annette Lavers and Colin Smith, Hill and Wang, New York, 1968, p 63.
[9]   Roland Barthes, *Mythologies*, translated by Annette Lavers, Harper Collins, London, 1973, p 11.

sign must be part of a system, he considered all objects equally worthy of this kind of meticulous textual analysis. Barthes' idea that we are always somehow locked within various networks of representation anticipated Derrida's famous notion that there is "nothing outside the text". Barthes provided a demonstration of the importance of these cultural "texts" – including works of architecture – and he tried to describe in his later writings the tools by which these texts could be "read". As he described in his essay on cities, given as a lecture in 1967:

> Here we rediscover Victor Hugo's old intuition: the city is a writing. He who moves about the city, e.g. the user of the city (what we all are), is a kind of reader who, following his obligations and his movements, appropriates fragments of the utterance in order to actualise them in secret.[10]

This dynamic engagement with the city, which he compared with the reading of modernist literature, provided a mechanism by which Barthes claimed it was possible to counteract society's myths. One of those he set out to attack was the literary opposition between reader and author, where the writer is the "creator" of meanings that the passive reader merely receives and deciphers. As the city is a collage of fragments, so too was writing in the modernist sense, and Barthes saw the enlightened reader as a dynamic agent in the interpretation process. In his famous essay "The Death of the Author", written in 1968, he describes the "instability" of meaning that results:

> We know now that a text is not a line of words releasing a single 'theological' meaning (the message of the Author-God) but a multi-dimensional space in which a variety of writings, none of them original, blend and clash. The text is a tissue of quotations drawn from the innumerable centres of culture.[11]

---

[10] Roland Barthes, "Semiology and the Urban", in Neil Leach (ed.), *Rethinking Architecture*, Routledge, London, 1997, p 170.

[11] Roland Barthes, "The Death of the Author", in *Image-Music-Text*, translated by Stephen Heath, Noonday Press, New York, 1988, p 146.

This implies that each act of speech is in some sense a repetition – that our words have always been spoken before us, and that language speaks "through us", as even Heidegger had suggested.

Barthes' thinking, however, is based on Saussure's idea of the arbitrariness of the sign, which allows the notion of the "free-play" of meaning to disrupt such "totalising" discourses as "reason, science and law".[12] It is here that Barthes is echoing a major theme in deconstruction, one that Derrida had already instigated in *Of Grammatology* in 1967. As Barthes describes it in the same essay, with the emphasis again on syntactic "structures":

> In the multiplicity of writing, everything is to be disentangled, nothing deciphered; the structure can be followed, 'run' (like the thread of a stocking) at every point and at every level, but there is nothing beneath: the space of writing is to be ranged over, not pierced; writing ceaselessly posits meaning ceaselessly to evaporate it, carrying out a systematic exemption of meaning.[13]

For Barthes it seemed that a deterministic structuralism could itself become just another myth and he wished to question its restrictive assumptions, such as its reliance on binary oppositions. This theme extends into deconstruction as part of what we now refer to as post-structuralist thinking, which builds on, rather than dismisses, the earlier philosophy – contrary to what the misleading label suggests. Other fields in which structuralism has found favour are touched on in Chapter 5 of this book, including two of Levi-Strauss' "three mistresses" – Marxism and psychoanalysis.

---

[12] Roland Barthes, "The Death of the Author", in *Image-Music-Text*, translated by Stephen Heath, Noonday Press, New York, 1988, p 147.
[13] Roland Barthes, "The Death of the Author", in *Image-Music-Text*, translated by Stephen Heath, Noonday Press, New York, 1988, p 147.

Semiotics in Architecture – The Rediscovery of Meaning

Where does all this leave us in terms of structuralism and the "language" of architecture? A possible connection was of course suggested by Barthes' use of the city as a metaphor. However, the more specific question of the building as a system of signs related to functions was left to the Italian writer Umberto Eco who wrote a lengthy essay on this topic. Eco was close to the work of Barthes with his interest in the sign-systems of everyday life, particularly the presence of archetypal themes in the narratives of popular culture. In a study from 1973, following the US President Nixon's fall from office, Eco set out an intriguing analysis of the narrative structure of Nixon's resignation speech. The essay was called "Strategies of Lying" and compared the speech with the pattern of a fairytale, tabulating its characters and episodes as Levi-Strauss had done with the Oedipus myth.[14]

In his essay devoted to buildings, "Function and Sign: The Semiotics of Architecture", Eco considered the more ambiguous problem of how an architectural element "signifies" its function. He began by dividing the question into primary and secondary functions which relate to the distinction adopted in linguistics between denotative and connotative meanings. The former refers to the literal meaning, or what the word denotes or "says", whereas the latter involves the more implicit references that are suggested by the manner of the saying. In everyday language the denotative is dominant, such as in the communication of facts or information, while the connotative becomes important in the case of poetic language, where information is of secondary concern. This division, however, oversimplifies the issues, as in reality the two categories coexist – as language is never a truly neutral means of communication, the poetic dimension will always intrude. Eco acknowledges this situation in another essay on architecture, on the 1967 Expo World Fair, where he describes the pavilions as reversing conventional functions, as the connotative takes over from the denotative. The normal relationship between primary and secondary – or between

[14] Claude Lévi-Strauss, "The Structural Study of Myth", in *Structural Anthropology*, Basic Books, New York, 1963, pp 206–31.

functional and symbolic form – is inverted in the case of the Expo pavilions, as they have no function except to symbolise their sponsors. This conclusion is based on the earlier definition of an architectural sign as denoting a function, such as the example of a staircase whose literal meaning would be the possibility of walking up it or down it. The principal theme that emerges in Eco's writing on architecture recalls Barthes' idea of the "free-play" of signifiers – the interpretation of buildings can never be controlled by the designer, just as the author cannot predetermine the reader's reading. Eco finally recommends that the architect must design for "variable primary functions and open secondary functions"[15], in the hope of inviting the user's creative engagement, or reappropriation, as Barthes had recommended with language.

Notwithstanding any ambiguity in the translation from language to architecture, these ideas have had a huge influence on architectural theory. Fundamentally, this thinking showed a new concern for the role of the interpreter, previously neglected in the modernist emphasis on functional norms. Rather than analysing user requirements and letting technology take care of the rest, the 1960s saw the reappearance of the question of meaning – a concern with how buildings were understood by their inhabitants and the role of history in this process of interpretation. A series of important books appeared from a variety of different sources that addressed a similar shortcoming in mainstream modernism. This consisted of a perceived poverty of expression in architectural form, resulting in a lack of engagement between buildings and their users. The first of these books, *Complexity and Contradiction in Architecture*, was written by Robert Venturi, and set out to reassess the lessons of history in architecture which he felt had been suppressed within modernism. *The Architecture of the City*, written by the Italian Aldo Rossi, also appeared in 1966. In this book urban form was considered as a series of historical layers, based on

---

[15] Umberto Eco, "Function and Sign: The Semiotics of Architecture", in *The City and the Sign*, Gottdiener and Lagapoulous (eds), Columbia University Press, New York, 1986, pp 56–85. Reprinted in Neil Leach (ed.), *Rethinking Architecture*, Routledge, London, 1997, p 200.

successive transformations of "archetypal" buildings. Rossi's book was only translated into English in 1982, but his work had in the meantime become internationally famous. *The Architecture of the City* had appeared in Spanish and German in the early 1970s, around the same time as another landmark work, what became the book *Collage City* written by Colin Rowe and Fred Koetter, which appeared as a journal article in 1975. This work also looked at traditional cities as a palimpsest of layers, as Roland Barthes had suggested in his analysis of literature.

The historical depth that all these writers were searching for in architecture was disappearing from the new "functional city" and their intention was not just to preserve it but to reinvent it as a method for making new buildings in the contemporary context. The effect of this reassessment of the principles of modernism was to open the way for linguistics in architecture – the possibilities for readdressing the relations between form and meaning were taken up with great interest around this time.

A good summary of this process was provided by Geoffrey Broadbent in his essay published in *Architectural Design* in 1978. Entitled "A Plain Man's Guide to the Theory of Signs in Architecture", the piece contained a systematic treatment of the field's major figures, along with explanations of their competing terminologies. He made a distinction between the two main areas of influence in architecture, using Saussure's division between syntactic and semantic. He described how the two fields might be pursued independently of each other, leading to contrasting expressions of form. The first, the syntactic view of architecture, with its emphasis on structures, is dismissed as a hermetic activity – the preoccupation with the rules of formal combination is seen as ignoring what buildings actually *mean*. The shortcomings of this criticism will be considered later in more detail, but for the moment it is worth noting Broadbent's conclusion. He regards the semantic dimension of language as inescapable for architecture, as even so-called neutral structures will inevitably carry meaning.

One of the first manifestations of this semantic tendency in architecture was the collection of essays published in 1969, entitled

Meaning and Architecture and edited by Charles Jencks and George Baird. Jencks went on to champion the use of semantic references in buildings, which became the basis of what we now refer to as the "language" of postmodernism in architecture. Robert Venturi was perhaps the first architect to make explicit use of these ideas, in terms of the self-conscious "quotation" of historic forms in his buildings. While in his early work from the 1960s these references are still fairly abstract – such as in the arch form across the doorway of the house for his mother, near Philadelphia – in his later work they appear in a much more literal form, as in the classical pilasters and Egyptian decoration of his Sainsbury Wing of the National Gallery in London. Uniting these two extremes is the principle of the arbitrariness of the sign, which in his written work Venturi had translated into an intriguing architectural theory. On the basis that any object could be made to signify a particular use, he saw a problem in the modernist principle of expressing a function through a specific form. Illustrated by his famous sketch of the "duck" and the "decorated shed", Venturi showed how a building could signify without resorting to functionalist expression. Rather than trying to make the form of the building express the character of what goes on inside, Venturi advocated the application of signs, as seen in his studies of Las Vegas hotels. He felt that modernism had compromised itself by insisting on functionalist expression and it was time to learn from commercial architecture in its techniques of communication:

> By limiting itself to strident articulations of the pure architectural elements of space, structure and program, modern architecture's expression has become a dry expressionism, empty and boring – and in the end irresponsible. Ironically, the modern architecture of today, while rejecting explicit symbolism and frivolous appliqué ornament, has distorted the whole building into one big ornament. In substituting 'articulation' for decoration, it has become a duck.[16]

To get over what he claimed was a problem within modernism of functional *expression* compromising functional *operation*, he tried to

[16] Robert Venturi *et al.*, *Learning From Las Vegas*, MIT Press, Cambridge, MA, 1997, p 103.

1 Venturi and Rauch – Franklin Court, Philadelphia, 1973–76. (Neil Jackson)

2 Robert Venturi and Denise Scott Brown – Sainsbury Wing, National Gallery, London, 1986–91. (Neil Jackson)

satisfy both demands by disconnecting them from each other, hence the functional "shed" and its expressive "decoration". This strategy involved a kind of honesty in its separation of the two functions and has led to a series of buildings characterised by their surface articulation – Venturi accepts that the architect often controls only the building's skin, so he treats it as a screen for the display of surface pattern. The more recent buildings at Princeton, such as Wu Hall from the early 1980s, and the ISI Building in Philadelphia, from 1978–79, show the implications of this approach to the decoration of surface. Another building which plays with the concept of the "empty" signifier is the Benjamin Franklin Museum which stands on the site of his former house. Instead of rebuilding the house from historical records, an outline of its form has been created in white-painted steel. This is an extreme example of a building that tries to deny its own substance,

3 Robert Venturi and Denise Scott Brown – Wu Hall, Princeton University, 1980–83. (Neil Jackson)

4 Robert Venturi and Denise Scott Brown – Research laboratories, Princeton University, 1986. (Alistair Gardner)

5 Venturi, Rauch and Scott-Brown – Institute for Scientific Information, Philadelphia, 1978–79. (Alistair Gardner)

making great play of the fact that it is merely trying to refer to something else.

The problem with this reduction of architecture to decoration is that people still have to inhabit the internal spaces of the "shed". Another architect who has also tried to make sense of this dilemma, and who shares the concern with history expressed by Venturi, is fellow American Michael Graves. Graves became known in the 1970s as one of the famous New York Five, after the book *Five Architects* published in 1972. At this stage, paradoxically, his work showed pronounced "syntactic" tendencies, being for the most part a revival of 1920s modernist forms. Beginning with the abstract geometric language of Le Corbusier's "purist" villas, Graves was just beginning to experiment by adding colour and fragmenting forms.

Following a period of study in Rome at the American Academy and the phenomenological influence of his colleague Peter Carl, his buildings also began to include more obviously figurative elements, along with the explicit quotation of historical references. In the essay accompanying his work, published in 1982, he made use of the language analogy to illustrate his interest in meaning. By distinguishing between the everyday and the poetic dimensions of language, he was also echoing Broadbent's division between syntactic and semantic:

> When applying this distinction of language to architecture, it could be said that the standard form of building is its common or internal language – determined by pragmatic, constructional and technical requirements. In contrast, the poetic form of architecture is responsive to issues external to the building, and incorporates the three-dimensional expression of the myths and rituals of society.[17]

Graves went on to admit that both dimensions of meaning are essential, but he concentrates on the latter as a reaction to its neglect in mainstream modernism. This poetic, or external, language is depend-

---

[17] Michael Graves, "A Case for Figurative Architecture", in Wheeler, Arnell and Bickford (eds), *Michael Graves: Buildings and Projects 1966-81*, Rizzoli, New York, 1982, pp 11-13. Reprinted in Kate Nesbitt (ed.), *Theorising a New Agenda for Architecture: An Anthology of Architectural Theory 1965-95*, Princeton Architectural Press, Princeton, 1996, pp 86-90.

6 Michael Graves – Humana
Building, Louisville, Kentucky,
1982–86. (Jonathan Hale)

7 Michael Graves – Humana
Building, Louisville, Kentucky,
1982–86. (Jonathan Hale)

ent on associational readings, where both figurative and anthropo-
morphic references are of major significance.

Graves blamed the lack of this kind of reference for the alienation
of modernist space, as he claimed that buildings no longer acted as
mediators between human beings and their environment:

> All architecture before the modern movement sought to elaborate the
> themes of man and landscape. Understanding the building involves both
> association with natural phenomena (for example, the ground is like the
> floor), and anthropomorphic allusions (for example, a column is like
> a man). These two attitudes within the symbolic nature of building
> were probably originally in part ways of justifying the elements of
> architecture in a pre-scientific society. However, even today, the same
> metaphors are required for access to our own myths and rituals within
> the building narrative.[18]

[18] Michael Graves, "A Case for Figurative Architecture", in Kate Nesbitt (ed.), *Theorising
a New Agenda for Architecture: An Anthology of Architectural Theory 1965-95*,
Princeton Architectural Press, Princeton, 1996, p 88.

8 Michael Graves – San Juan Capistrano Library, California, 1982.
(Neil Jackson)

9 Michael Graves – San Juan Capistrano Library, California, 1982.
(Neil Jackson)

The fact that building elements are nameable objects, such as arch, column and floor, meant that they were also memorable to the building user as a way of establishing a sense of place. Graves felt this quality had been lost in the abstractions of modernist geometries, where points, lines and planes no longer allowed this kind of reading. The shortcomings in Graves' buildings, however, result from a different kind of abstraction, where the abrupt shifts of scale disrupt conventional expectations. The curious combination of historical quotations, whose volumetric quality is denied by the thinness of their construction, results in a feeling of superficial unreality that belies the gravity of Graves' theoretical position.

Semantics or Syntactics? – The Meaning of Structures

There is a distant echo in Graves' thinking of some phenomenological themes and it is perhaps no surprise to find Norberg-Schulz writing positively of Graves' work.[19] In an essay on figurative architecture, published in 1985, he claimed that many ideas in postmodernism were actually implicit within modernism. On the issue of materiality, however, this comparison appears tenuous, as the understanding of Graves' work is predominantly visual and intellectual – a consequence of the structuralist principle of the "immateriality" of the sign. Another way of interpreting a possible continuity with modernism is to return to the syntactic analysis of the language of architecture. It is perhaps here among the work of a group of late-modernists that the future potential of linguistics might still become apparent. In fact, one of the earliest manifestations of structuralist thinking in architecture emerges within modernism in the work of Aldo van Eyck. The Dutch architect, educated in England, has written widely on his work and was part of the Team X group of post-war architects that were mentioned in Chapter 1. In the 1950s van Eyck and the Team X group were heavily critical of the modernist city and its tendency to erase the past. Rather than preserving ancient fabrics for the sake of sentiment or nostalgia, van Eyck attempted to draw out the underlying principles of traditional forms. By identifying the common characteristics in the architectures of the past he hoped to arrive at a "synchronic" series of timeless formal principles:

> Man after all has been accommodating himself physically in this world for thousands of years. His natural genius has neither increased nor decreased during that time. It is obvious that the full scope of this enormous environmental experience cannot be combined unless we telescope the past. . . . I dislike a sentimental antiquarian attitude toward the past as much as I dislike a sentimental technocratic one toward the future. Both are founded on a static, clockwork notion of time (what anti-

---

[19] Christian Norberg-Schulz, "On the Way to Figurative Architecture", in *Architecture: Meaning and Place, Selected Essays*, Rizzoli, New York, 1988, pp 233–45.

quarians and technocrats have in common) so let's start with the past for a change and discover the unchanging condition of man.[20]

Van Eyck boiled down these formal principles into the concept of "twin-phenomena", which echoes Saussure's analysis of language as being fundamentally a system of differences. In van Eyck's case these differences were based on the qualities of architectural space and were defined as a series of binary terms with contrasting characteristics. These included open-closed, dark-light, inside-outside, solid-void and unity-diversity, all of which, van Eyck maintained, should be seen as inseparable pairs. Architecture should act as the mediator, keeping the dualities in "equipoise":

> All twin-phenomena together form the changing fabric of this network – and the constituent ingredients of architecture. Though different, each of them, they are at the same time - this is the point - also reciprocally open to each other. Far from being mutually exclusive or independent, they merge, lean on each other. Equality is their cardinal common denominator. Their very essence is in fact, complementary, not contradictory.[21]

Perhaps the best illustration of van Eyck's structuralist method is the orphanage he designed on the outskirts of Amsterdam, completed in 1960. The building shows the possibilities of van Eyck's "syntactic" approach to architecture, where a complexity of spaces results from a comparatively small number of components. The basic modules that have been developed to satisfy the accommodation requirements are repeated and rearranged to create an interesting hierarchy of spaces. Circulation routes and spaces are made to overlap around doorways and the inside–outside theme is also evident in the use of courtyards and full-height glazing.

---

[20] Aldo van Eyck, "The Interior of Time", in *Forum*, July 1967, pp 51-4. Quoted in Kenneth Frampton, *Modern Architecture: a Critical History*, Thames and Hudson, London, 1992, p 298.
[21] Aldo van Eyck, "Building a House" in Herman Hertzberger *et al.*, *Aldo van Eyck*, Stichting Wonen, Amsterdam, 1982, p 43.

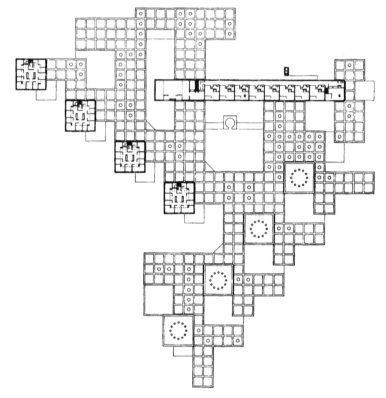

10 Aldo van Eyck – Orphanage, Amsterdam, 1957–60: Upper level plan.
(Redrawn by the author, after Aldo van Eyck)

Due to the repetition of its constructional elements and the strong
aesthetic of repeated units, the scheme still retains the mass-produced
quality of many of the early modernist "industrialised" buildings. This
problem has been addressed by a former colleague of van Eyck, fellow
Dutch architect Herman Hertzberger, who was heavily influenced by
structuralist thinking. The key issue for Hertzberger was the problem
of engaging with the building user and how to prevent the feeling of
alienation implied by the abstract language of syntactic structures. In
the Centraal Beheer office building built in 1974, he adopted a similar
approach to van Eyck's orphanage in developing a structural module
as a repeatable unit. The units accommodate a series of open-plan

11 Aldo van Eyck – Hubertus House for Single Mothers, Amsterdam, 1973–78. (Alistair Gardner)

offices which are laid out on a tartan grid, but the real success of the spaces themselves depends on the way in which they are interpreted by the building's users:

> What we must look for in place of prototypes which are collective interpretations of individual living patterns, are prototypes which make individual interpretations of the collective patterns possible.[22]

At Centraal Beheer the basic structure is seen as a "language system" which allows flexibility in its interpretation, whereas individual acts of

---

[22] Herman Hertzberger, quoted in Kenneth Frampton, *Modern Architecture: a Critical History*, Thames and Hudson, London, 1992, p 299.

12 Aldo van Eyck – Hubertus House for Single Mothers, Amsterdam, 1973–78. (Alistair Gardner)

13 Herman Hertzberger – LiMa Housing, Berlin-Kreuzberg, 1982–86.
(Alistair Gardner)

14 Herman Hertzberger – Centraal Beheer Offices, Apeldoorn, The
Netherlands, 1968–72. (Alistair Gardner)

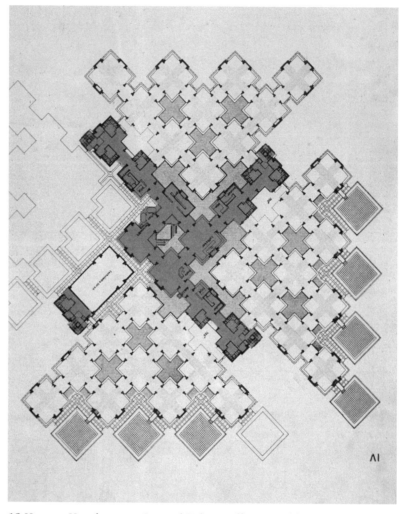

15 Herman Hertzberger – Centraal Beheer Offices, Apeldoorn, The Netherlands, 1974: Upper level plan. (Redrawn by the author, after Herman Hertzberger)

"speech" take place when specific activities begin to colonise a space. Likewise at the Utrecht Music Centre where Hertzberger employs a similar analogy for his column system, although here the architecture is made more expressive in its elaboration of the basic unit:

The column system forms a minimum system of arrangement that allows great freedom when it comes to filling it in, and that is able to coordinate the large variety of parts issuing from the highly complex program. While ensuring the unity of the whole, the column system is an encouragement to shape every spot according to the requirements of each particular situation.[23]

By this means he hoped to engender a sense of identity between user and space, based on the "colonisation" of the individual's environment, which the building itself sets out to encourage. To assist this process of appropriation a series of clues is provided by the architect – places to sit, to display objects and the use of modularised furniture which can be moved around are all attempts to inspire involvement between the often passive inhabitant and his/her physical environment. While Michael Graves had opted for a semantic solution, offering familiar forms and historical references, Hertzberger had proposed a more open and dynamic process of bodily engagement through the building's use. That patterns of use engender meanings has already been mentioned in our discussion of language, but with the elements of architecture the same could be argued, as did Roland Barthes with the Eiffel Tower. He saw the Tower as a raw piece of technology which acted as an idealised "empty" sign – an ideal model of the "neutral" signifier to which various meanings could easily attach themselves. Barthes model of the "active" reader – engaged in a creative process of reinterpretation – could also be applied to Hertzberger's ideal inhabitant, as a kind of *bricoleur* effectively remaking the building.

Another alternative to Graves' semantic version of structuralist thinking came from his fellow New York Five members, Richard Meier and Peter Eisenman. Meier has gone on to develop his approach based on an abstract geometry of "white" forms through a series of larger scale projects for museum and gallery buildings, such as the Atheneum

---

[23] Herman Hertzberger, "Building Order" in *VIA*, No. 7, 1984, p 41. Revised version included in Herman Hertzberger, *Lessons for Students in Architecture*, translated by Ina Rike, Uitgeverij 010, Rotterdam, 1991, pp 126–45.

16 Gustave Eiffel – Eiffel Tower, Paris, 1889. (Alistair Gardner)

17 Richard Meier – Atheneum, New Harmony, Indiana, 1975–79. (Jonathan Hale)

18 Richard Meier – High Museum of Art, Atlanta, 1980–83. (Jonathan Hale)

19 Richard Meier – High Museum of Art, Atlanta, 1980–83: Interior
circulation (Jonathan Hale)

at New Harmony and the High Museum in Atlanta. While these later works dealt with movement and the idea of the "architectural promenade" they held back from a truly rigorous engagement with the disciplines of syntactic structures. Eisenman, on the other hand, makes explicit use of these ideas, such as in the complex formal systems and transformations in "House VI". The basic principle in Eisenman's work is similar to that seen with Hertzberger, where the meaning of the form is initially somewhat arbitrary, but while in Hertzberger's case significance arises out of use-patterns, in Eisenman's work it is even more elusive. Where "meaning follows function" in Hertzberger's buildings, "function follows form" with Eisenman. As he writes of it himself in describing "House I" in the essay included in the book *Five Architects*:

> House I posits one alternative to existing conceptions of spatial organisation. Here there was an attempt, first, to find ways in which form and space could be structured so that they produce a set of formal relationships which is the result of the inherent logic of the forms themselves, and, second, to control precisely the logical relationships of those forms.[24]

He goes on to discuss the distinction in architecture between the real structure of the building and the implied structure of form – the latter providing a potentially "deep-structural" system which he claims might provide new potential to receive meanings.

Throughout these early projects he considers architecture as an autonomous discipline and explores the code by which forms are combined. This syntax then generates a series of transformations which forms a system of compositional principles. As one critic wrote in describing this process:

> Eisenman's early work thus incorporates two standard structuralist principles: the bracketing off of the context, both physical and historical,

[24] Peter Eisenman, "Cardboard Architecture", in *Five Architects: Eisenman, Graves, Gwathmey, Hejduk, Meier*, Oxford University Press, New York, 1975. Partially reprinted in *Theories and Manifestoes of Contemporary Architecture*, Jencks and Kropf (eds), Academy Editions, London, 1997, p 241.

and, with that, the bracketing off of the individual subject, in favour of a notion of an intersubjective architectural system of signification that, like language, pre-dates any individual and is much less his or her product than he or she is the product of it.[25]

Hence the difficulty for the outsider in interpreting Eisenman's code, as the language is inevitably internal to the discipline. By the same token, as the philosopher Andrew Benjamin has pointed out,[26] this notion of pre-existing "impersonal" structures is a key component of the idea of tradition. By actively engaging with the very history of the discipline at this deeper and most universal of levels, Eisenman is potentially producing a more meaningful kind of discourse, based as it is on architecture's fundamental components.

It is here where poststructuralism, in its reassessment of these ideas, intersects with deconstruction in terms of its engagement with tradition. As Eisenman's architecture begins to show, in its abstract formal language, there is still much to be gained from an understanding of "deep structures" of form. This theme of underlying forces and how they influence our understanding will resurface again in Chapter 5 and this book's conclusion – firstly as a component of the political analysis of buildings and finally as part of the general field of interpretation.

Suggestions for further reading

Background

Roland Barthes, *Mythologies*, translated by Annette Lavers, Harper Collins, London, 1973.

Terry Eagleton, "Structuralism and Semiotics", in *Literary Theory: An Introduction*, University of Minnesota Press, Minneapolis, 1983, pp 91–126.

---

[25] K. Michael Hays, "From Structure to Site to Text: Eisenman's Trajectory", in *Thinking the Present: Recent American Architecture*, Hays and Burns (eds), Princeton Architectural Press, New York, 1990, p 62.

[26] See Chapter 2.

Richard Kearney, "Ferdinand de Saussure", "Claude Lévi-Strauss" and "Roland Barthes", in *Modern Movements in European Philosophy*, Manchester University Press, Manchester, 1986.

Claude Lévi-Strauss, "The Structural Study of Myth", in *Structural Anthropology*, Basic Books, New York, 1963, pp 206–31.

Ferdinand de Saussure, *Course in General Linguistics*, translated by Wade Baskin, McGraw-Hill, New York, 1966.

Foreground

Roland Barthes, "Semiology and the Urban", in Neil Leach (ed.), *Rethinking Architecture*, Routledge, London, 1997, pp 166–72.

K. Michael Hays, "From Structure to Site to Text: Eisenman's Trajectory", in *Thinking the Present: Recent American Architecture*, Hays and Burns (eds), Princeton Architectural Press, New York, 1990, pp 61–71.

Herman Hertzberger, "Building Order" in *VIA*, No. 7, 1984 revised version included in Herman Hertzberger, *Lessons for Students in Architecture*, pp 126–45, translated by Ina Rike, Uitgeverij 010, Rotterdam, 1991.

Charles Jencks, *The Language of Post-Modern Architecture*, Academy Editions, London, 1978.

Robert Venturi *et al.*, *Learning from Las Vegas*, MIT Press, Cambridge, MA, 1997.

Readings

Geoffrey Broadbent, "A Plain Man's Guide to the Theory of Signs in Architecture", in *Architectural Design*, No. 47, 7-8/1978, pp 474–82. Reprinted in Kate Nesbitt (ed.), *Theorising a New Agenda for Architecture: An Anthology of Architectural Theory 1965-95*, Princeton Architectural Press, New York, 1996, pp 124–40.

Mario Gandelsonas, "Linguistics in Architecture", in *Casabella*, No. 374, 2/1973. Reprinted in K. Michael Hays (ed.), *Architecture Theory Since 1968*, MIT Press, Cambridge, MA, 1998, pp 114–22.

Michael Graves, "A Case for Figurative Architecture", in Wheeler,

Arnell and Bickford (eds), *Michael Graves: Buildings and Projects 1966-81*, Rizzoli, New York, 1982, pp 11-13. Reprinted in Kate Nesbitt (ed.), *Theorising a New Agenda for Architecture: An Anthology of Architectural Theory 1965-95*, Princeton Architectural Press, New York, 1996, pp 86-90.

5

POLITICS AND ARCHITECTURE
The Marxist Tradition

As we saw in Chapter 4 the inspiration for the structuralist method was the search for the deeper forces that affect our understanding. According to Lévi-Strauss, the great propagandist of structuralist ideas, his particular motivation grew from three distinctly different sources – the disciplines of geology, Marxism and psychoanalysis. The common thread linking all three is the fundamental principle that what appears on the surface is controlled by deeper forces from within. In this chapter the latter two fields will be discussed in relation to architecture, and the connections with structuralist thinking will become significant in several ways. Three important thinkers in the philosophical development of the twentieth century have all worked with structuralist principles in their own particular disciplines: Louis Althusser on the structures of ideology, Jacques Lacan on the structures of the unconscious and Michel Foucault on the structures of power. All three philosophers were born in France and all three died in the 1980s.

To appreciate further the significance of these connections between disciplines, it will be important to understand the broader background to these issues; firstly, the question of politics and its underlying influence on architectural theory, for which we will have to look back to the philosophical "revolution" of the nineteenth century; and secondly, the notion of the unconscious and its unseen influence on our social behaviour, and particularly the way psychoanalysis has been taken up in a political context. While the two fields seem separate when briefly summarised in this way, the underlying themes that could be said to link them should become apparent on closer study.

A major theme in the traditional debate over the relationship between architecture and society is the political potential of art in general as a means of critique or social comment. As we saw in Part 1, the view of architecture as a creative art could be seen as an implied critique of technological determinism – a protest at the reduction of architecture to the impoverished practice of "shelter-engineering". In a more specifically political sense this chapter will consider the status of architecture in society in relation to the dominant political paradigm of the Western capitalist liberal democracy. Under the present system a great deal of political power seems to lie with the vast multinational corporations, as they threaten to engulf the world with a "culture" of blandness and uniformity. Companies like the Disney Corporation, Coca Cola and Sky TV are fast becoming the great new world powers, as they expand their influence across the globe and threaten the survival of local cultures. In this context, social responsibility usually involves resistance to these globalising forces, although all varieties of ideological "distortion" are seen as targets for the political artist.

From Marx to Marxism

The school of thought that today believes in the critical capacity of the work of art – for exposing the underlying structures of political control and economic power – still for the most part draws its theoretical model from the work of Karl Marx, in addition to its various reworkings by his more recent interpreters. The key issue is the idea of architecture as a mode of "resistance" and transformation, with the power to effect change through its direct impact on the environment. As Marx pointed out, in one of his earliest writings: "Philosophers have only *interpreted* the world, in various ways; the point, however, is to *change it.*"[1] To begin to understand the work of Marx and the reason for his significant and lasting influence, it is necessary to consider a few of his key concepts before discussing their broader impact.

In approaching Marx's philosophy it is important to understand his situation in history, as a student in Berlin in the aftermath of Hegel's dominating influence. Marx arrived in Berlin in 1836, just five years after the great philosopher had died. Hegel had been teaching in Berlin as a professor of philosophy since 1818 and had left a huge and lasting legacy which the next generation now had to deal with. For Marx and a group of colleagues who called themselves the Young Hegelians, the emphasis was on trying to locate the weak points in the great edifice of Hegel's system. We have seen in Chapter 1 how Hegel had constructed a historical philosophy which presented the whole course of history as the quest for absolute knowledge. Hegel had shown the force behind this process to be the emerging "world-spirit", an "idea" attempting to express itself in the physical forms of the visible world. The culmination of Hegel's history took place in the mind of the philosopher, being the ultimate manifestation of "spirit" as it comes to its own self-understanding. This idealism has gone down in history as one of Hegel's grandest conceptions and it is this great historical principle that soon attracted Marx's attention.

Rather than tinker with the minutiae in attempting to refine Hegel's system, Marx set out to attack its foundations by questioning its most basic assumptions. He dismissed philosophical history as a dry academic abstraction, cut off from the real history of everyday conditions and experience:

> The Hegelian philosophy of history is the last consequence, reduced to its 'finest expression', of all this German historiography, for which it is not a question of real, nor even of political, interests, but of pure thoughts, which consequently must appear to Saint Bruno, as a series of 'thoughts' that devour one another and are finally swallowed up in 'self-consciousness'.[2]

---

[1] Karl Marx, *Theses on Feuerbach*. Reprinted in *The Marx-Engels Reader*, Robert C. Tucker (ed.), Norton & Company, New York, 1978, p 145.
[2] Karl Marx and Friedrich Engels, *The German Ideology*. Reprinted in *The Marx-Engels Reader*, Robert C. Tucker (ed.), Norton & Company, New York, 1978, p 166.

It was consciousness that became the great pivot-point for Marx, about which he tried to turn Hegel's philosophy on its head, although more accurately he described it as standing Hegel on his feet. He felt that the idealist approach had tried to build a philosophy from ideas, while he was attempting to reverse this and build an alternative from experience. Hegel had, according to Marx, simply inverted the real course of history, so to correct this Marx constructed a system more closely modelled on reality. He did borrow, however, Hegel's dialectical model, where progress is described as an interplay between consciousness and reality. Where in Hegel this process leads to a refinement of concepts, with Marx it transforms the material conditions of reality. In Marx's terms this amounted to a "dialectical materialism", although he himself only ever referred to it as the "materialist conception of history". As he wrote in 1859, in one of his few philosophical works to be published during his lifetime:

> The mode of production of material life conditions the social, political, and intellectual life-process in general. It is not the consciousness of men that determines their being, but, on the contrary, their social being that determines their consciousness.[3]

Marx seemed to suggest that as individuals we are restricted in our actions due to the presence of an unseen structure that appears to limit the mind's potential for free thinking. In a model comparable to the structuralist conception of the underlying systems of language, Marx set out the means by which this deterministic process might take place:

> In the social production of their life men enter into definite relations that are indispensable and independent of their will, relations of production which correspond to a definite stage of development of their material productive forces. The sum total of these relations of production consti-

---

[3]   Karl Marx, Preface to *A Contribution to the Critique of Political Economy*. Reprinted in *The Marx-Engels Reader*, Robert C. Tucker (ed.), Norton & Company, New York, 1978, p 4.

tutes the economic structure of society, the real foundation, on which rises a legal and political superstructure and to which correspond definite forms of social consciousness.[4]

This is the now classic description of the "base and superstructure" model, depicting the geological conception of history that Claude Lévi-Strauss was so enamoured with. The base consists of two components, firstly the "forces of production", being the raw materials, machinery and labour required for producing industrial goods. The second part he called the "relations of production", referring to the ways in which the work is organised, such as in the typical pyramidal structure of the capitalist corporate hierarchy.

The superstructure which rises out of this base and which is, in Marx's terms, determined by it, consists of the social, political and legal institutions that make up the society's "consciousness". Quite how deterministic Marx meant this model to be is still the subject of much argument among scholars. Marx does, however, suggest a direct link between the two components of the base, when he says "the hand-mill will give you a society with the feudal lord, the steam-engine a society with the industrial capitalist".[5] This presents a slightly caricatured version of Marx's thinking on the process of history which, in the case of the base and superstructure relationship, was more complex than first appears. In fact the reasoning behind Marx's call for philosophers to change the world lies with the problem caused by one section of society being exploited by another. In Marx's model the class that controls the base thereby also controls the superstructure, and under capitalism this meant the working classes being locked into their relations of production. With the institutions of the superstructure being controlled by the bourgeoisie, this meant that the workers were prevented from gaining any understanding of their exploitation. Various corollaries to this scenario soon followed in Marx's thinking, as he set out

---

[4]   Karl Marx, Preface to *A Contribution to the Critique of Political Economy*. Reprinted in *The Marx-Engels Reader*, Robert C. Tucker (ed.), Norton & Company, New York, 1978, p 4.

[5]   Quoted in David McLellan, *Karl Marx*, Penguin, New York, 1975, p 40.

the possibilities for revolution based on his analysis of historical progress. He saw that in the civilisations of the past a particular society would tend to collapse when the "contradictions" within the system had broken out onto the surface. As he wrote at the beginning of his famous work, *The Communist Manifesto*:

> The history of all hitherto existing societies is the history of class struggles. Freeman and slave, patrician and plebeian, lord and serf, guildmaster and journeyman, in a word, oppressor and oppressed, stood in constant opposition to one another, carried on an uninterrupted, now hidden, now open fight, a fight that each time ended, either in a revolutionary re-constitution of society at large, or in the common ruin of the contending classes.[6]

Besides the continuing exploitation of one class by another, in modern society a new danger had arisen inside the system. As a consequence of the division of labour within the capitalist mode of production, the new industrialised worker had now become "alienated" from his work. By breaking up industrial processes into a series of specialised components, capitalism had robbed ordinary workers of any meaningful connection with their work. As Marx somewhat lyrically described it, referring to a previous system of production:

> Supposing that we had produced in a human manner; each of us would in his production have doubly affirmed himself and his fellow men. I would have objectified in my production my individuality and its peculiarity and thus both in my activity enjoyed an individual expression of my life and also in looking at the object have had the individual pleasure of realising that my personality was objective, visible to the senses and thus a power raised beyond all doubt.[7]

---

[6]   Karl Marx and Frederick Engels, *The Communist Manifesto*, Eric Hobsbawm (ed.), Verso, London, 1998, pp 34–5.
[7]   Karl Marx, *Economic and Philosophical Manuscripts*. Quoted in David McLellan, *Karl Marx*, Penguin, New York, 1975, pp 31–2.

The real importance of this process is as part of the worker's "self-creation", where the personality of the producer is invested in their product – this existentialist idea also anticipates the work of William Morris, the pioneer English socialist and leader of the Arts and Crafts movement. Instead, the industrial product has become a mere anonymous commodity, prized for its "exchange–value" rather than any "use-value" in itself, and the worker, at the same time, becomes commodified under this sytem, valued as a labour resource rather than a unique human being.

Not surprisingly, perhaps, Marx's political views brought him into early conflict with academia and even his work as a journalist was soon suppressed by the Prussian state. In 1843 he moved to Paris in search of more progressive surroundings, where he met a fellow German, Friedrich Engels, who became his lifelong collaborator. Engels, who had been working in his family's textile business in Manchester, gave Marx some first-hand experience of capitalism, as well as much-needed financial support. In Paris his radical journalism met with further opposition from the government and he was forced to move to Brussels until the onset of the German revolution of 1848. By this time he had written the famous *Communist Manifesto* for the Communist League he had helped establish there. The revolution in Germany collapsed in 1849 and he then moved back from Cologne to Paris before finally settling down to live in London. It was only after his death in 1883 that his more famous philosophical writings began to appear in print, with the exception of the first volume of his study of *Capital* which he did see published in 1867.

Though Marx accepted that capitalism had produced many benefits for society, such as much greater prosperity through an increase in productivity, he saw no reason for the unfair "relations of production", where a minority seemed at liberty to exploit the labour of the majority. As a final stage in the development of an "ideal" society, one without class divisions or destructive "antagonisms", he predicted a social revolution that would resolve these contradictions and create a new system of common ownership of the means of production:

The monopoly of capital becomes a fetter upon the mode of production, which has sprung up and flourished along with, and under it. Centralisation of the means of production and socialisation of labour at last reach a point where they become incompatible with their capitalist integument. This integument is burst asunder. The knell of capitalist private property sounds.[8]

The remaining difficulty for Marx's theory was explaining why this revolution had not taken place – why the conflicting elements in society were being held together in equilibrium. He came up with the concept of "ideology" to explain why this was the case, and it is here that Marx's base and superstructure model becomes a good deal more refined – although he also falls back on a metaphor, in one of his earlier formulations:

> If in all ideology men and their circumstances appear upside-down as in a *camera-obscura*, this phenomenon arises just as much from their historical life-process as the inversion of objects on the retina does from their physical life-process . . . The phantoms formed in the human brain are also, necessarily, sublimates of their material life-process, which is empirically verifiable and bound to material premises. Morality, religion, metaphysics, all the rest of ideology and their corresponding forms of consciousness, thus no longer retain the semblance of independence.[9]

This "false consciousness" as Engels called it is promoted by the institutions of the superstructure, which ensure that the contradictions within society are accepted as immutable natural principles – thus a dominant mythology supports the status quo (much as Roland Barthes described it in Chapter 4). This mythology serves to suppress the two great conflicts in society – between the worker and the product, which has now become an "alien" object, and between the individual and the community, due to the laws of private property – and this pre-

---

[8] Karl Marx, *Capital,* Volume 1. Reprinted in *The Marx-Engels Reader,* Robert C. Tucker (ed.), Norton & Company, New York, 1978, p 438.
[9] Karl Marx and Friedrich Engels, *The German Ideology.* Quoted in David McLellan (ed.), *The Thought of Karl Marx,* Macmillan, London, 1995, p 159.

vents, according to Marx, the workers' consciousness of their exploitation; thus the revolutionary impulse is never allowed to break through.

The concept of ideology shows the dialectical nature of Marx's thinking, and provides the necessary refinement to the deterministic model of history. The issue centres on his intention to change, rather than merely interpret, the conditions of society, with the question now being, where do you begin – to change consciousness or to change conditions? According to Marx's more humanistic earlier writings, it is the former activity that becomes a priority for the philosopher. Seeing beyond the ideological "illusion" that prevents awareness of political injustice also becomes a major theme in later Marxist thinking – centred on the question of cultural activity as a means of exposing ideology to the process of critique.

Marxist Interpretation – Lukács, Gramsci and Benjamin

Marx's early works only began to appear in print around 1930, with his *Economic and Philosophical Manuscripts* making most impact. One writer who had anticipated some of the themes contained in these early writings was the Hungarian philosopher and literary critic, Georg Lukács. Lukács contested the empirical, "scientific" interpretation of Marxism that had been promoted by Engels following Marx's death. Anticipating Thomas Kuhn, on the principle of the paradigm, he writes:

> The blinkered empiricist will of course deny that facts can only become facts within the framework of a system – which will vary with the knowledge desired. He believes that every piece of data from economic life, every statistic, every raw event already constitutes an important fact. In so doing he forgets that however simple an enumeration of 'facts' may be, however lacking in commentary, it already implies an 'interpretation'.[10]

---

[10] Georg Lukács, *History and Class Consciousness: Studies in Marxist Dialectics*, translated by Rodney Livingstone, Merlin Press, London, 1971, p 5.

This kind of mechanical understanding meant the laws of society had come to be accepted as beyond man's control, whereas Lukács restored the importance of the concept of alienation as a way of explaining how this ideological illusion had come about. In his *History and Class Consciousness* (1923), he attempted to reinterpret Marx in terms of the philosophy of Hegel, by reinstating the creative role of the collective human consciousness. He coined the term "reification" (meaning "turning into a thing") to explain what happens to human consciousness in the alienating conditions of modern industrial capitalism. This idea mirrors Marx's concept of the "fetishisation" of commodities, where an analogous process of transformation occurs in reverse. In Marx's terms, the product of alienated labour takes on an almost magical existence of its own, like the fetish-objects used in many archaic religious rituals, which were endowed with quasi-human capabilities. When the product enters the market place it acquires its own exchange–value and enters into a "society" of relations with other commodities. Marx saw this as elevating the object above humanity, at the same time as the worker was reduced from a human being to a commodity.

Lukács used this notion to explain how Marxism itself had been distorted as later writers had reduced the human element in Marx's thinking. Instead of the inevitable revolution that Marx had seemed to forecast, based on the inexorable growth of new conditions leading to a necessary change of consciousness, Lukács reinstated the dialectic between the two terms, with the responsibility for change resting on the shoulders of the workers:

> The truth that the old intuitive, mechanistic materialism could not grasp turns out to be doubly true for the proletariat, namely that it can be transformed and liberated only by its own actions, and that the 'educator must himself be educated'. The objective economic evolution could do no more than create the position of the proletariat in the production process. . . . But the objective evolution could only give the proletariat the opportunity and the necessity to change society. Any transformation can only come about as the product of the - free - action of the proletariat itself.[11]

[11] Georg Lukács, *History and Class Consciousness: Studies in Marxist Dialectics*, translated by Rodney Livingstone, Merlin Press, London, 1971, pp 208-9.

A further refinement of the "vulgar" Marxist understanding of history came from the Italian philosopher, Antonio Gramsci, who was also active in the Communist party around the time of World War 1. Following the failure of the Communists to take power after the war, Gramsci was imprisoned by the Fascists in the late 1920s. While detained he was allowed to write, and composed a series of *Prison Notebooks*, which were published after his death following his release in 1937. Gramsci's contribution to Marxist thinking echoes that of Lukács, although he develops the problem of ideology into the field of popular culture. He uses the concept of *hegemony* to describe the pervasive presence of ideology, and to explain why Marx's "base and superstructure" notion is too simplistic when taken literally. Again he develops a dialectical relationship between the two components of Marx's model, and shows how the institutions of the superstructure actually serve to support the base. This takes place at the level of ideas, through the process of dissemination carried on by the state which, by controlling the supply of information, is able to condition a great deal of what people think. According to Gramsci, class interests present themselves as cultural phenomena and it is these in turn that become reified into seemingly "natural" principles. This second nature that is created, as a cocoon around society, prevents anyone seeing outside it to a possible alternative system. As he wrote in the *Prison Notebooks* on the "educative" role of the state:

> . . . One of its most important functions is to raise the great mass of the population to a particular cultural and moral level, a level (or type) which corresponds to the needs of the productive forces for development, and hence to the interests of the ruling classes. The school as a positive educative function, and the courts as a repressive and negative educative function . . . (and) in reality, a multitude of other so-called private initiatives and activities tend to the same end – initiatives and activities which form the apparatus of the political and cultural hegemony of the ruling classes.[12]

---

[12] Antonio Gramsci, *Selections from the Prison Notebooks*, translated by Hoare and Nowell-Smith, Lawrence and Wishart, London, 1971, p 258.

Another radical thinker to suffer persecution by the Fascists was the German writer Walter Benjamin, forced to flee to Paris in the 1930s. Benjamin also worked with Marxist themes in the context of popular culture, conducting a detailed study of the Parisian arcades as vehicles of nineteenth century commodity capitalism. As Susan Buck-Morss explained in her book on the unfinished Arcades Project:

> . . . the key to the new urban phantasmagoria was not so much the commodity-in-the-market as the commodity-on-display, where exchange-value no less than use-value lost practical meaning, and purely representational value came to the fore. Everything desirable, from sex to social status, could be transformed into commodities as fetishes-on-display that held the crowd enthralled even when personal possession was far beyond their reach. Indeed, an unattainably high price-tag only enhanced a commodity's symbolic value.[13]

At the same time, with the arcades a new architecture had evolved in iron and glass, which eroded the distinction between inside and outside space. This perfectly suited the status of the new "commodity fetish", which relied on a similar breakdown between consumer and consumed – the disorientation at work in the new space of the arcade served to support this confusion between subject and object. For Benjamin this was exemplified in the figure of the prostitute, a characteristic combination of seller and product.

Another inhabitant of the arcades who became important in Benjamin's thinking was the *flâneur*, or urban "wanderer" who resisted the temptations of consumption by his ceaseless window-shopping and seemingly aimless movement. Benjamin appropriated this kind of activity as a model of resistance to commodification, suggesting that as the *flâneur* assembles impressions of the city, the artist should assemble "found" objects. He took this approach himself, in his work on the Arcades Project, and he describes it in his own words as:

[13] Susan Buck-Morss, *The Dialectics of Seeing: Walter Benjamin and the Arcades Project*, MIT Press, Cambridge, MA., 1989.

. . . the attempt to capture the portrait of history in the most insignificant representations of reality, its scraps as it were.[14]

In his essay on the philosophy of history he took a similarly radical view, recommending the revision of the grand narratives – or the "history of the victors" – in favour of the "forgotten" history of ordinary lives:

> According to traditional practice, the spoils are carried along in the procession. They are called cultural treasures, and a historical materialist views them with cautious detachment. For without exception the cultural treasures he surveys have an origin which he cannot contemplate without horror. They owe their existence not only to the great minds and talents who have created them, but also to the anonymous toil of their contemporaries. There is no document of civilisation which is not at the same time a document of barbarism.[15]

In Benjamin's conception of an alternative writing of history, the popular culture of the arcades would have played a significant role. There is also a nagging ambiguity, however, in much of Benjamin's thinking, between a nostalgia for the traditional "crafts", such as storytelling, painting and theatre, and the excitement at the prospect of a liberating politics being ushered in by the new arts of photography and cinema. This is especially evident in what is perhaps his single most famous essay, "The Work of Art in the Age of Mechanical Reproduction".

The Critique of the "Culture Industry" – Ideology and the Frankfurt School

In contrast to Benjamin's studies of "low-cultural" resistance, and Gramsci's active involvement with Communist politics at party level,

---

[14] Walter Benjamin, *Illuminations*, translated by Harry Zohn, Schocken Books, New York, 1968, p 11.
[15] Walter Benjamin, "Theses on the Philosophy of History", in *Illuminations*, translated by Harry Zohn, Schocken Books, New York, 1968, p 256.

the work of the Frankfurt School provides an alternative, more abstract approach, with its strategy of theoretical analysis and an emphasis on "high-cultural" critique. The Institute for Social Research (as it was originally titled) started life in Frankfurt in 1923, although it soon moved from Germany following Hitler's rise to power, to restart at Columbia University in New York. The leading figures in the Frankfurt School (who incidentally supported Benjamin with the payment of a stipend and the offer of teaching in New York) were Max Horkheimer and Theodor Adorno – as mentioned in Chapter 1, discussing the "ideology" of functionalism in architecture. Adorno's studies in modernist music and his general interest in avant-garde culture left him unsympathetic to the critical possibilities of more populist forms of art. This is in marked contrast to Walter Benjamin, with whom he frequently argued on this point, who rated the accessibility of a Charlie Chaplin film over the obscurity of a Dadaist performance.

Adorno and Horkheimer collaborated on an important work entitled the *Dialectic of Enlightenment*, which extended the debate on ideology begun by Lukács and Gramsci. They were also inspired by the writings of the sociologist Max Weber and his work on the historical development of what he called the "capitalist spirit". Weber had claimed the origin of capitalism lay in the Protestant work ethic, the doctrine of selfless asceticism preached by northern European churches. This has led, according to Weber, to the triumph of rationality in the quest for efficiency above all other concerns:

> Now the peculiar modern Western form of capitalism has been, at first sight, strongly influenced by the development of technical possibilities. Its rationality is today essentially dependent on the calculability of the most important technical factors. . . . On the other hand, the development of these sciences and the technique resting upon them, now receives important stimulation from these capitalistic interests in its practical economic application.[16]

---

[16] Max Weber, *The Protestant Ethic and the Spirit of Capitalism*, translated by Talcott Parsons, Routledge, London, 1992, p 24.

The "iron cage" of modernity that Weber was attacking was also the target of Adorno and Horkheimer, in terms of its basis in enlightenment rationality. In their book, they described the workings of what they termed the "culture industry", where enlightenment had become "mass-deception" through the products of technological culture. Where Hollywood movies, pulp fiction, popular music and so on are all produced under the aegis of capitalist financing and marketing systems, any form of resistance is prevented from ever reaching a mass audience by the mechanisms which are set up to distribute the dominant messages. As they describe it, this homogenisation is driven ultimately by technical imperatives:

> Interested parties explain the culture industry in technological terms. It is alleged that because millions participate in it, certain reproduction processes are necessary that inevitably require identical needs in innumerable places to be satisfied with identical goods. The technical contrast between the few production centres and the large number of widely dispersed consumption points is said to demand organisation and planning by management. . . . The result is the circle of manipulation and retroactive need in which the unity of the system grows ever stronger.[17]

To try to escape this manipulation they recommended the strategy of "negation" and "transcendence", where the former involved a critique of the system and the latter an attempt to see beyond it.

To step outside the process of conditioning is the fundamental problem for the radical philosopher; how to prevent any revolutionary thinking being merely absorbed within the present system. If there is no "Archimedean point" from which a neutral observer can merely observe – uncontaminated by the distorting filter of ideological influence upon their thinking – how can a strategy of resistance begin to suggest alternative ways of living, and thereby succeed in persuading the masses to demand the changes necessary to achieve it? Another member of the Frankfurt School who tried to address this intractable

---

[17] Theodor W. Adorno and Max Horkheimer, *Dialectic of Enlightenment*, translated by John Cumming, Verso, London, 1979, p 121.

problem was the German philosopher Herbert Marcuse, who also despaired of the "culture industry". As he wrote in *One-Dimensional Man* (1964), which also had a great influence on the student protests a few years later:

> The means of mass transportation and communication, the commodities of lodging, food and clothing, the irresistable output of the entertainment and information industry carry with them prescribed attitudes and habits, certain intellectual and emotional reactions which bind the consumers more or less pleasantly to the producers and, through the latter, to the whole. The products indoctrinate and manipulate; they promote a false-consciousness which is immune against its falsehood.[18]

Marcuse, in his earlier work, had also combined these Marxist themes with a reworking of various ideas he had discovered from his study of psychoanalysis. Beginning with the pioneering work of the Viennese doctor, Sigmund Freud, Marcuse developed the notion of the *unconscious* into a tool of political analysis. In the effort to decode ideologies and escape their insidious influence, Freud's "topological" model of the human psyche provided another possible mechanism. As Lévi-Strauss had indicated by his comparison of "geology, Marxism and psychoanalysis", the base–superstructure model of Marxism was mirrored in Freud's diagram of the structure of the mind. The unconscious–conscious split was modified in Freud's later work to become a three-part system of relations between *super-ego*, *ego* and *id*. The id, or "it", at the base, is seen as the primordial source of our instincts and these are repressed by the authority of the super-ego to prevent them from upsetting the "social" functioning of the ego (or "I" – the conscious self). This domination of the instinctual desires by the action of the super-ego involves a process of repression that echoes that of the capitalist system over the worker. The psychological process of internalisation of the childhood figures of authority, such as when the mature adult's "super-ego" stands in for the absent parent, appears to

---

[18] Herbert Marcuse, *One-Dimensional Man: Studies in the Ideology of Advanced Industrial Society*, Beacon Press, Boston, 1991, p. 12.

prepare the individual ego for the relations of domination within society, and to repress the individual instinct for freedom and liberation.

In Freud these repressed desires re-emerge in alternative guises, such as in dream images, "Freudian" slips of the tongue, or, more seriously, in neuroses. In *Eros and Civilisation* Marcuse attempted a psychoanalysis of capitalism, identifying what he called a repressed life-impulse ("eros") forced into the service of capitalist production. This was a more general application of what Weber had described as the Protestant work ethic behind the success of capitalism, but it carried with it the implication that repressed desires might once again be unleashed. The realm in which these desires could be expressed was, for Marcuse, that of artistic activity, where images of a non-repressive society might yet inspire the kind of revolution needed to fulfil them. As he wrote, quoting Adorno, on art as a realm of critique:

> Art is perhaps the most visible 'return of the repressed', not only on the individual but also on the generic–historical level. The artistic imagination shapes the 'unconscious memory' of the liberation that failed, of the promise that was betrayed. . . . Art opposes to institutionalised repression 'the image of man as a free subject; but in a state of unfreedom art can sustain the image of freedom only in the negation of unfreedom'.[19]

This positive conclusion on the function of art in the Frankfurt School's thinking on ideology was further supported by Marcuse's later book *The Aesthetic Dimension* which was published in 1978, the year before his death.

Ideology in France – Althusser, Foucault and Debord

Of the more recent attempts to come to terms with ideology, not all have remained faithful to Marx's thinking – in particular the work of the French philosopher Michel Foucault, who was a student of Louis

---

[19] Herbert Marcuse, *Eros and Civilisation: A Philosophical Inquiry into Freud*, Routledge, London, 1987, p 144.

Althusser. Althusser had tried to redefine ideology as solely a result of material practices, taking the opposite, "scientific" view of Marx from that of the Frankfurt School, seeing him purely as a materialist philosopher. Ideology, for Althusser, did not originate with ideas, but rather at the level of inherited structures, like language, and this was to a large extent due to the influence of structuralist thinking. This view had a significant impact on the understanding of the human subject, who was reduced to a transient "effect" of these pre-existing structures – as Barthes and Derrida had already begun to suggest, the individual is always locked within these various networks of representation.

It was this "construction" of the subject through the action of larger forces that attracted the interest of Foucault, who became obsessed with the study of institutional practices and the surreptitious exercise of power. He was determined to identify in the concrete evidence of history the "inscription" of these impositions of power and he did this through the study of knowledge, as well as institutions such as hospitals and prisons. This is how he described his work, looking back on his career:

> My work has dealt with three modes of objectification which transform human beings into subjects. The first is the modes of enquiry which try to give themselves the status of sciences; for example, the objectivising of the speaking subject in *grammaire générale*, philology and linguistics . . . In the second part of my work, I have studied the objectivising of the subject in what I call 'dividing practices'. The subject is either divided inside himself or divided from others . . . Examples are the mad and the sane, the sick and the healthy, the criminals and the 'good boys'. Finally, I have sought to study . . . the way a human being turns him, or herself, into a subject. For example I have chosen the domain of sexuality – how men have learned to recognise themselves as subjects of 'sexuality'. . .[20]

Foucault takes great pains to re-problematise these oppositions, to show how they are artificially constructed to appear as "natural" prin-

---

[20] Michel Foucault, "The Subject and Power", quoted in Richard Kearney, *Modern Movements in European Philosophy*, Manchester University Press, Manchester, 1986, pp 296-7.

ciples – much as poststructuralism has attempted to do with the binary oppositions of structuralism, as a way of opening up the possibilities of meaning.

In Foucault's earlier work he also questioned the view of history as a linear development and suggested instead a model of change through "epistemological breaks" – similar to Thomas Kuhn's notion of scientific paradigms, though applied at a more general level across the field of knowledge as a whole. In his later writing he considered the place of the individual subject within the institutionalised power-relations of society. His description of the all-encompassing presence of power in society is reminiscent of the Marxist definitions of ideology (although he vehemently denied any specifically Marxist sympathies, as he also denied subscribing to the structuralist school of thought):

> Power's condition of possibility . . . is the moving substrate of forced relations which, by virtue of their inequality, constantly engender states of power, but the latter are always local and unstable. The omnipresence of power: not because it has the privilege of consolidating everything under its invincible unity, but because it is produced from one moment to the next, at every point, or rather in every relation from one point to another. Power is everywhere not because it embraces everything, but because it comes from everywhere.[21]

A concrete example of this process in action comes in his essay on the "Panopticon", the building devised by Jeremy Bentham, the eighteenth century prison reformer. This theatre-like circular structure with an outer ring of prisoners' cells could be policed from a central watch tower, by a single person able to see all round. The sensation of being under surveillance meant that the inmates would "police" themselves and thus the very fabric of the building itself ensured the efficient operation of the disciplinary system. Foucault uses the example of the Panopticon as an extreme case of a general phenomenon, such as he sees in other institutional buildings such as hospitals, factories

---

[21] Michel Foucault, *The History of Sexuality, Volume I: An Introduction*, translated by Robert Hurley, Vintage Books, New York, 1990, p 93.

and schools. As he describes it in *Discipline and Punish*, his influential book from 1975:

> This was the problem of the great workshops and factories, in which a new type of surveillance was organised. . . . what was now needed was an intense, continuous supervision; it ran right through the labour process; it did not bear – or not only – on production (the nature and quality of raw materials, the type of instruments used, the dimensions and quality of its products); it also took into account the activity of the men, their skill, the way they set about their tasks, their promptness, their zeal, their behaviour.[22]

Foucault sees this process of imposing a generalised disciplinary order as part of the organisation of cities as well as individual buildings. As he pointed out in a later interview, published as "Space, Knowledge and Power", this process began to become formalised at the end of the eighteenth century:

> One begins to see a form of political literature that addresses what the order of a society should be, what a city should be, given the requirements of the maintenance of order; given that one should avoid epidemics, avoid revolts, permit a decent and moral family life, and so on. In terms of these objectives, how is one to conceive of both the organisation of a city and the construction of a collective infrastructure?[23]

Against Althusser's materialism Foucault is willing to admit that there is still a dialectical relationship between objects and ideas. This is important in his thinking on the status of architecture, and the interplay between buildings and the spatial practices they accommodate.

Later in the interview that was quoted above, he was asked about the relationship between architecture and freedom:

---

[22] Michel Foucault, *Discipline and Punish: The Birth of the Prison*, translated by Alan Sheridan, Vintage Books, New York, 1995, p 174.

[23] Michel Foucault, "Space, Knowledge and Power", interview with Paul Rabinow. Reprinted in Neil Leach (ed.), *Rethinking Architecture*, Routledge, London, 1997, pp 367-68.

I do not think it is possible to say that one thing is of the order of 'liberation' and another is of the order of 'oppression'. . . . a concentration camp . . . is not an instrument of liberation, but one should still take into account – and this is not generally acknowledged – that, aside from torture and execution, which preclude any resistance, no matter how terrifying a given system may be, there always remain the possibilities of resistance, disobedience and oppositional groupings.

And at the same time, freedom cannot be guaranteed by the physical form of buildings either:

The liberty of men is never assured by the institutions and laws that are intended to guarantee them. This is why almost all of these laws are capable of being turned around. . . . I think that it can never be inherent in the structure of things to guarantee the exercise of freedom. The guarantee of freedom is freedom.

Having said this, Foucault does preserve a vital role for the creativity of the architect, when the liberating intentions of the designer "coincide with the real practice of people in the exercise of their freedom".[24]

On this issue of practice as a mode of resistance to ideology, the French thinker, Guy Debord, also made a decisive contribution. Debord returned to the problem of reification as set out by Lukács, to develop a remarkable set of observations on the state of society in the 1960s. Published as *Society of the Spectacle* in 1967, the book had a direct impact on political activities as well as a more enduring influence on later Marxist thinking. Debord extended Lukács' notion of the commodity as fetish – the phenomenon of workers reduced to "objects" and objects become alive with "magical" qualities – to suggest that a further stage of confusion between the realms of the ideal and the material had resulted from the "image" of the commodity coming to dominate instead:

[24] Michel Foucault, "Space, Knowledge and Power", interview with Paul Rabinow. Reprinted in Neil Leach (ed.), *Rethinking Architecture*, Routledge, London, 1997, pp 371-2.

This is the principle of *commodity fetishism*, the domination of society by 'intangible as well as tangible things', which reaches its absolute fulfillment in the spectacle, where the tangible world is replaced by a selection of images which exist above it, and which at the same time are recognised as the tangible *par excellence*.[25]

As part of Debord's resistance to this condition he formed the Situationist International, a group of writers and artists committed to new modes of experience, which produced the journal of the same name in the late 1950s and through the 1960s. Alongside the spontaneous reappropriations of public space, such as in performance-art "happenings", which they referred to as "situations", they were also influenced by Benjamin's description of the *flâneur* and developed the "Theory of the Dérive" in response to this idea:

> Among the various situationist methods is the *dérive* [literally: 'drifting'], a technique of transient passage through varied ambiences. The *dérive* entails playful-constructive behaviour and awareness of psychogeographical effects.[26]

The paradoxical role that vision plays in the understanding of "psychogeography" has led more recent French critics to take a less condemning view of the image. Jean Baudrillard in particular has become fascinated by the "autonomy" of the sign and the way in which sign value has taken precedence over exchange value. In his early work he combined a Marxist approach with Saussure's analysis of the sign, to show how the spectacle of "image consumption" had grown out of the detachment of *signifier* from *referent*. In his later writings he went on to celebrate this new culture of "simulation", although without the political agenda of his earlier, more critical work.

---

[25] Guy Debord, *Society of the Spectacle*, Black and Red, Detroit, 1983, §36.
[26] Guy Debord, "The Theory of the Dérive", *Internationale Situationniste*, No. 2, December 1958. Reprinted in Ken Knabb (ed.), *Situationist International Anthology*, Bureau of Public Secrets, Berkeley, CA, 1981, p 50.

The Marxist Critique in Architecture – Tafuri and Jameson

The various modes of resistance that we have discussed so far towards the dominant power structures and institutions of society would not necessarily be ones that all architects would agree with – even, paradoxically, the ones most politically engaged. The Italian historian, Manfredo Tafuri, who was deeply influenced by Marxist ideas, doubted that architects on their own could achieve very much in the absence of a general revolution in society. As he wrote in an essay from 1969 which was later expanded into the book *Architecture and Utopia*, he felt that the social intentions of architecture seen in the Utopian projects of early modernism had been co-opted by the all-pervading machinery of capitalism. He blamed this on the ideology of instrumental rationality, much as Adorno and Horkheimer had previously done, as this was part of the enlightenment origin of modernism that had "naturalised" the basic principles of capitalism. Architectural practice today could not escape this hegemony, and would always end up colluding with the progress of the capitalist project, therefore the only positive role for an architecture that was opposed to this ideology was not in the world of practice but in the realm of critique:

> It may even be that many marginal roles exist for architecture and planning. Of primary interest to us however, is the question of why, until now, Marxist-oriented culture has very carefully, and with an obstinacy worthy of better causes, denied or concealed the simple truth that, just as there can be no such thing as a political economics of class, but only a class critique of political economics, likewise there can never be an aesthetics, art or architecture of class, but only a class critique of aesthetics, art, architecture and the city.[27]

On a more positive note, Tafuri does recognise the potential of the "critical" architectural project to point to an alternative mode

---

[27] Manfredo Tafuri, "Toward a Critique of Architectural Ideology", *Contropiano* I, January–April 1969. Reprinted in K. Michael Hays (ed.), *Architecture Theory Since 1968*, MIT Press, Cambridge, MA, 1998, p 32.

febb. 74.

Architettura assassinata _ AR _

1 Aldo Rossi – "Architettura Assassinata", 1974–75

of practice. In the introduction to the book version of the essay quoted above, he does take care to deny the charge of forecasting the "death of architecture" – implied by Aldo Rossi's famous drawing made in response to the original publication. In fact he comes down in support of more "autonomous" architecture – such as was discussed in Chapter 2 of this book, in terms of a critique of rationality – though here employed as the only alternative now that capitalism has disempowered a revolutionary architecture:

> What is of interest here is the precise identification of those tasks which capitalist development has taken away from architecture. That is to say what it has taken away in general from prefiguration. With this, one is led almost automatically to the discovery of what may well be the 'drama' of

2 Paolo Soleri – "Arcosanti", Arizona, 1969 onwards. (Neil Jackson)

architecture today: that is, to see architecture return to pure architecture, to form without utopia; in the best cases to sublime uselessness.[28]

At this point Tafuri's argument could be compared with our earlier conclusion on the critical capacity of architecture as discussed in Chapter 2. Tafuri, at the same time, seems reluctant to admit that while this may be effective against an architectural ideology, this should not be confused with ideology in general:

> To the deceptive attempts to give architecture an ideological dress, I shall always prefer the sincerity of those who have the courage to speak of that silent and outdated 'purity'; even if this, too, still harbours an ideological inspiration, pathetic in its anachronism.[29]

In contrast to this pessimistic conclusion, the Marxist critic Fredric Jameson has recently offered a more hopeful response. He has specifi- cally tried to transcend Tafuri's "peculiarly frustrating position"[30] and propose a more positive agenda for architecture as a means of orienta- tion within the homogenised environment of a global "late-capitalism". Jameson borrowed a notion from Kevin Lynch's book *The Image of the City* in order to develop a political version of what Lynch had termed the technique of "cognitive mapping". This originated from research on how people construct mental maps in order to navigate particular routes and areas within confusing urban environments. To Jameson this became a way of describing a possible Marxist aesthetic, whereby political opposition might be similarly orientated within the hegemony of capitalism:

> . . . in which we may again begin to grasp our positioning as individual and collective subjects and regain a capacity to act and struggle which is

[28] Manfredo Tafuri, *Architecture and Utopia: Design and Capitalist Development*, translated by Barbara Luigia La Penta, MIT Press, Cambridge, MA, 1976, p ix.
[29] Manfredo Tafuri, *Architecture and Utopia: Design and Capitalist Development*, translated by Barbara Luigia La Penta, MIT Press, Cambridge, MA, 1976, p ix.
[30] Fredric Jameson, "Is Space Political", in Cynthia Davidson (ed.), *Anyplace*, MIT Press, Cambridge, MA. Reprinted in Neil Leach (ed.), *Rethinking Architecture*, Routledge, London, 1997, p 259.

at present neutralised by our spatial as well as our social confusion. The political form of postmodernism, if there ever is any, will have as its vocation the invention and projection of a global cognitive mapping, on a social as well as a spatial scale.[31]

Jameson likewise imagined the Utopian project to be a key component of this "counterhegemony", suggesting alternative ideas and practices of space against which society could develop new demands of the present system. It is here that his thinking overlaps most directly with Tafuri, although at the same time he also refers back to Marx's writings – particularly the way the new emerges from within the old:

> Such figures suggest something like an *enclave* theory of social transition, according to which the emergent future . . . is theorised in terms of small yet strategic pockets or beach-heads within the older system. The essentially *spatial* nature of the characterisation is no accident and conveys something like a historical tension between two radically different types of space, in which the emergent yet more powerful kind will gradually extend its influence and dynamism over the older form, fanning out from its initial implantations and gradually 'colonising' what persists around it.[32]

Towards a Marxist Practice – Lefebvre and De Certeau

The theme of revolution at the small scale – almost by stealth as opposed to sudden transformation – has also been a powerful influence in grass roots architectural practice, as part of a movement to democratise the process. As a contrast to the critique implied by the "pure architecture" mentioned by Tafuri, discussed at the end of Chapter 2 and returned to in Chapter 4, this section will conclude with

---

[31] Fredric Jameson, *Postmodernism, or, The Cultural Logic of Late-Capitalism*, Verso, London, 1991, p 54.
[32] Fredric Jameson, "Architecture and the Critique of Ideology", in Joan Ockman (ed.), *Architecture, Criticism, Ideology*, Princeton Architectural Press, Princeton, 1985. Reprinted in K. Michael Hays (ed.), *Architecture Theory Since 1968*, MIT Press, Cambridge, MA, 1998, p 453.

a brief illustration of another approach towards the problems of political change. The notion of direct action in order to change conditions
– as opposed to the Utopian strategy of beginning with a revolution in
consciousness – has resulted in various attempts by architects to act as
intermediaries or "enablers", reorganising the process of building
through community participation. The philosophical background to
this approach can be found in various sources, particularly the French
tradition of political activism which became significant during the student revolts of the late 1960s.

Henri Lefebvre is perhaps the most intriguing of those directly
involved with the French student protests and his major work, *The
Production of Space*, shows the implications of his grass roots activity. There is a richness and complexity in Lefebvre's thinking due to a
wide range of philosophical influences, particularly his innovative
combination of phenomenological and Marxist themes, which gave his
work a strong connection to everyday life. His major target was what
he called "abstract space" which he felt modern architecture had produced under capitalism, and he was likewise critical of postmodernist
semiotics which he felt relied too heavily on purely visual imagery. As
the critic Michael Hays has written, introducing Lefebvre's work:

> Abstract space is at once fragmented and homogeneous; capitalism com-
> partmentalises and routinises all activity, . . . Such contradictions cause
> differences to assert themselves even as abstract space tends to dissolve
> all difference. And it is precisely the instability of abstract space that
> produces the potential to resist its domination, to produce an 'other'
> space, by what Lefebvre calls the 'appropriation' of space from its
> alienation in capitalism – 'the "real" appropriation of space, which is
> incompatible with abstract signs of appropriation serving merely to mask
> domination'.[33]

The kind of activity Lefebvre was referring to involved a shift of
architectural interest from the large scale of strategic planning to the

---

[33] K. Michael Hays, *Architecture Theory Since 1968*, MIT Press, Cambridge, MA, 1998,
p 175.

level of everyday "tactics". This difference was theorised more specifically in the work of Michel de Certeau, who was also influenced by Lefebvre's writing on everyday life, in the development of his notion (with reference also to Foucault) of an "anti-disciplinary" practice of resistance to authority:

> Many everyday practices (talking, reading, moving about, shopping, cooking, etc.) are tactical in character. And so are, more generally, many 'ways of operating'; victories of the 'weak' over the 'strong' (whether the strength be that of powerful people or the violence of things or of an imposed order, etc.), clever tricks, knowing how to get away with things, 'hunter's cunning,' . . . . The Greeks called these 'ways of operating' *metis*. But they go much further back, to the immemorial intelligence displayed in the tricks and imitations of plants and fishes. From the depths of the oceans to the streets of modern megalopolises, there is a continuity and permanence in these tactics.[34]

This idea of appropriation is described by de Certeau as a mode of resistance to the dominant practices of capitalism in modern society. This also parallels an idea of Barthes on the subversion of dominant discourses, and the ways in which the active reader reappropriates a text – as de Certeau would have it, reading as "poaching" – or meandering through a text like Benjamin's wandering *flâneur*. This technique of creative reading, which becomes almost an act of rewriting, is likened by de Certeau to the inhabitation of space, and he also connects this idea with improvisation in poetry:

> This mutation makes the text habitable, like a rented apartment. It transforms another person's property into a space borrowed for the moment by a transient. Renters make comparable changes in an apartment they furnish with their acts and memories; . . . as do pedestrians, in the streets they fill with their desires and goals. . . . The ruling order serves as a support for innumerable productive activities, while at the same time blinding its proprietors to this creativity . . . Carried to its limit this order

---

[34] Michel de Certeau, *The Practice of Everyday Life*, translated by Steven Rendall, University of California Press, Berkeley, CA, 1984, p xx.

3 Paolo Soleri – "Arcosanti", Arizona, 1969 onwards. (Neil Jackson)

would be the equivalent of the rules of metre and rhyme for poets of earlier times: a body of constraints stimulating new discoveries, a set of rules
with which improvisation plays.[35]

This notion of improvisation recalls the architectural intentions of
Herman Hertzberger, who also attempted to inspire this kind of engagement between buildings and their users. A more extreme example of

[35] Michel de Certeau, *The Practice of Everyday Life*, translated by Steven Rendall,
University of California Press, Berkeley, CA, 1984, pp xxi-xxii.

4 Christopher Alexander *et al.* – Sala House, Albany, California, 1982–85.
(Neil Jackson)

this can be seen in the involvement of users in design, and there are
several cases worth considering, particularly for their curiously similar
formal characteristics. These range from whole cities constructed by
their inhabitants, such as Paolo Soleri's monumental Arcosanti, down to
the one-off house built by the client, with the architect acting as an on-
site advisor. This latter scenario has been championed by Christopher
Alexander, who started life as a mathematician, and then went on to
analyse the process of design through a system of numerical variables.
In his later work this approach softened somewhat into the more flexible method of designing with *Patterns*, which he then developed into
a handbook or manual, which could be used by anyone to design a
building to their own requirements. At the Sala House in California this
was applied to a single family dwelling, but he has also worked on
larger scale developments, such as a college campus in Japan. In

5 Christopher Alexander *et al.* – Sala
House, Albany, California, 1982–85:
Interior. (Neil Jackson)

6 Christopher Alexander *et al.* – Sala
House, Albany, California, 1982–85:
Interior. (Neil Jackson)

discussing the Eishin campus, constructed in 1985, Alexander presents
the project as a kind of civil war between two competing systems of
building. The first – "world system A" – is based on his use of the
Pattern Language, and the second – "world system B" – the conventional, professionally organised, construction process.

> World system A is based on human feelings. It is engaged in trying to cre-
> ate a world in which human feeling comes first, . . . and in which whole-
> ness (and) rightness, . . . is the quality in the world, which embodies and
> depends on human feeling at every point. World system B is based on
> mechanical and unfeeling processes. It poses a world of money, oppor-
> tunity and power, in which ultimate things – wholeness and spirit – are
> relegated to a very distant place.[36]

[36] Christopher Alexander, "Battle: The History of a Crucial Clash Between World-System
A and World-System B", in *Japan Architect*, Tokyo, August 1985, p 35.

7 Christopher Alexander *et al.* – Mexicali Housing, Mexico, 1976. (Neil Jackson)

Aside from the questionably "spiritual" qualities that might be present in Alexander's architecture, in the context of modern Japan this project was seen as a threat to the economic system. In Alexander's words this confrontation takes on the scale of a heroic encounter, but it does show the consequences of any attempt to subvert the system:

> We see the Japanese (construction) companies aware, for the first time, of the fact that our intention to implement system A, might have serious consequences for their own future in Japan. What we were doing, . . . in its pure form posed a threat to the whole Japanese construction industry. . . . They therefore set out to ensure that it must fail.[37]

---

[37] Christopher Alexander, "Battle: The History of a Crucial Clash Between World-System A and World-System B", in *Japan Architect*, Tokyo, August 1985, p 19.

8 Christopher Alexander *et al.* – Mexicali Housing, Mexico, 1976. (Neil Jackson)

The project did in fact go ahead, amidst much acrimony and confusion, and the buildings achieved a level of craftsmanship not always attained in Alexander's work. His smaller scale projects by contrast often rely on self-build construction, such as the community housing project built for a small town in Mexico. This project was described in the book called *The Production of Houses* (1985), which formed a real "construction manual" as a counterpart to the earlier design guide. Throughout all this work the intention was to hand over the "means of production", such that the worker might be relieved of the alienation Marx had described. As yet there has been no larger scale "revolution" due to the lack of a mass response from the wealthy populations of the Western world.

This sort of project has also been carried out on various scales in Europe, such as in the work of the German architect, Frei Otto, and the

9 Frei Otto *et al.* – Okö House, Berlin, 1990. (Neil Jackson)

Austrian, Lucien Kroll. Both men have been concerned to encourage direct user-participation, leading to an architecture of often chaotic and somewhat over-complex forms. The individual involvement in design that these buildings encourage can be seen quite clearly in their visual expression, which becomes symbolic of the architect stepping back from control of production. As Kroll writes of his own work and its grand agenda, which is tempered at the same time with a degree of resignation:

> In order to create a type of politics unrealisable at present, we are trying out in advance the different methods which might one day bring about the political situation we have in mind. This is simply a question of suggesting prototypes . . . and of taking note of their possibilities or drawbacks. We have never imagined that we could bring about revolution

10 Frei Otto *et al.* – Okö House, Berlin, 1990. (Neil Jackson)

11 Ralph Erskine – Byker Wall Housing, Byker, Newcastle-upon-Tyne, 1969–80. (Alistair Gardner)

with pockets of alternative architecture, which, to make a revolutionary impact, would have to infiltrate the existing constraints.[38]

In Britain in the 1980s this approach gained a strong following under the banner of "community architecture", and with the sponsorship of the Prince of Wales. One of the best known and most successful examples of this is the Byker Wall housing in Newcastle, where an existing community was transplanted into a range of individually tailored house-types. Its architect, Ralph Erskine, part of the post-war Team X group, is still pursuing these methods in his later work alongside his other, ecological, concerns. The ongoing project for the Millenium Village at Greenwich in London, will perhaps be Erskine's last attempt to transform the provision of housing.

On the wider scale in architectural theory, a range of other "revolutionary" agendas have also come into prominence in the last ten years or so. In particular, the environmental movement, under the slogan of "green architecture", has again challenged the traditional priorities of capitalism with a new emphasis on ecological concerns. In a similar sense, a change of consciousness has also been sought on another level, in the emerging influence of feminist theory and the concept of "gendered space". A further parallel exists here with the agenda of previous political projects, in terms of a return of repressed forces which are now beginning to find a voice.

Quite how much architectural design can achieve by way of change – particularly with its emphasis on form as opposed to social context – throws up a whole series of questions concerning other interrelationships, which many philosophers have already suggested in their thinking. As Mary McLeod has pointed out in a controversial essay on this subject, it is the coincidence of many forces that must be manipulated to achieve an effect:

---

[38] Lucien Kroll, "Architecture and Bureaucracy", in Byron Mikellides (ed.), *Architecture for People: Explorations in a New Humane Environment*, Studio Vista, London, 1980, pp 162–3.

12 Ralph Erskine – Byker Wall Housing, Byker, Newcastle-upon-Tyne, 1969–80. (Jonathan Hale)

Both the historicist and the poststructuralist tendencies correctly pointed to the failures of the modern movement's instrumental rationality, its narrow teleology, and its overblown faith in technology, but these two positions have erred in another direction in their abjuration of all realms of the social and in their assumption that form remains either a critical or affirmative tool independent of social and economic processes. That contemporary architecture has become so much about surface image and play, and that its content has become so ephemeral, so readily transformable and consumable, is partially a product of the neglect of the material dimensions . . . - programme, production, financing and so forth - that more directly invoke questions of power. And by precluding issues of gender, race, ecology and poverty, postmodernism and deconstructivism have also forsaken the development of a more vital and sustained heterogeneity.[39]

This view implies that we are still caught up in the dilemma suggested by Le Corbusier, when in 1923 he presented architecture as an alternative to revolution.[40] It should be clear from the modes of resistance set out by recent Marxist philosophers that the real "revolutions" take place at the level of spatial practice. The strategy of subverting the dominant paradigms through the unofficial use of various tactics - such as improvising with "found" objects, technology transfer and "poaching" of spaces, as de Certeau remarked - provides a range of possibilities for the enlightened consumer to step outside the commodification process. The more the strategies of coercive advertising and media manipulation are exposed by political artists, commentators and critics, the more informed people might become in the choices they make regarding their economic and cultural conditions. As a method of criticism of the art and architecture produced under capitalist conditions, the contextual background to the particular work becomes of paramount importance to the Marxist view. However, as Foucault and Derrida have suggested in the notion of the cultural

---

[39] Mary McLeod, "Architecture and Politics in the Reagan Era: From Postmodernism to Deconstructivism", *Assemblage*, 8, February 1989. Reprinted in K. Michael Hays (ed.), *Architecture Theory Since 1968*, MIT Press, Cambridge, MA, 1998, p 696-7.

[40] Le Corbusier, *Towards a New Architecture*, translated by Frederick Etchells, Architectural Press, London, 1946, pp 268-9.

"text", all objects have a dual potential as modes of practice and modes of critique. The merging of theory and practice into a broader, more critical discipline, will be discussed in the conclusion of this book under the general heading of "hermeneutics".

Suggestions for further reading

Background

Walter Benjamin, *Illuminations: Essays and Reflections*, translated by Harry Zohn, Schocken Books, New York, 1968.

Michel de Certeau, *The Practice of Everyday Life*, translated by Steven Rendall, University of California Press, Berkeley, CA, 1984.

Guy Debord, *Society of the Spectacle*, Black and Red, Detroit, 1983.

Terry Eagleton, "Conclusion: Political Criticism", in *Literary Theory: An Introduction*, University of Minnesota Press, Minneapolis, 1983, pp 194-217.

David Hawkes, *Ideology*, Routledge, London, 1996.

Richard Kearney, "Georg Lukács", "Walter Benjamin", "Herbert Marcuse" and "Michel Foucault", in *Modern Movements in European Philosophy*, Manchester University Press, Manchester, 1986.

David McLellan, *Karl Marx*, Penguin Books, New York, 1975.

Karl Marx/Friedrich Engels, *The Marx-Engels Reader*, Robert C. Tucker (ed.), Norton, New York, 1978.

Foreground

Christopher Alexander, *The Production of Houses*, Oxford University Press, New York, 1985.

William McDonough, "Design Ecology, Ethics and the Making of Things" and "Hannover Principles", in Kate Nesbitt (ed.), *Theorising a New Agenda for Architecture: An Anthology of Architectural Theory 1965-95*, Princeton Architectural Press, New York, 1996, pp 400-10.

Mary McLeod, "Architecture and Politics in the Reagan Era: From Postmodernism to Deconstructivism", *Assemblage*, 8, February 1989. Reprinted in K. Michael Hays (ed.), *Architecture Theory Since 1968*, MIT Press, Cambridge, MA, 1998, pp 696-7.

Manfredo Tafuri, *Architecture and Utopia: Design and Capitalist Development*, translated by Barbara Luigia La Penta, MIT Press, Cambridge, MA, 1976.

John F. C. Turner, *Housing By People*, Marion Boyars, London, 1976.

Readings

Michel Foucault, "Space, Knowledge and Power", interview with Paul Rabinow. Reprinted in Neil Leach (ed.), *Rethinking Architecture*, Routledge, London, 1997, pp 367-79.

Fredric Jameson, "Architecture and the Critique of Ideology", in Joan Ockman (ed.), *Architecture, Criticism, Ideology*, Princeton Architectural Press, New York, 1985. Reprinted in K. Michael Hays (ed.), *Architecture Theory Since 1968*, MIT Press, Cambridge, MA, 1998, pp 442-61.

Conclusion

Towards a "Critical" Hermeneutics

The use of the word "hermeneutics" in the title of this conclusion is not meant to suggest another discipline which might replace all the others. Hermeneutics today is a problematic term because of its historical associations, but I am using it in the broadest sense to mean the general practice of interpretation. Chapters 1 and 2 of this book set out two contrasting schools of thought – two opposing views on the question of meaning in architecture. The first assumes that architecture has no meaning at all, except as a solution to the problem of providing convenient sheltered space. The second approaches architecture as a pure artistic exercise, with its priority to communicate a message rated above all other concerns.

Both positions do not, of course, exist in actuality. I have used these ideas rather as interpretive frameworks – lenses through which to consider various *tendencies*. The fact that they are only tendencies and that architecture is always less straightforward should have become clearer in the subsequent chapters on the various interpretive models. That buildings always carry messages, whether intentionally or not, renders architecture *representational* along with all human endeavours. As the theatre director Peter Brook wrote, on the origin of dramatic art:

> I can take any empty space and call it a bare stage. A man walks across this empty space whilst someone else is watching him, and this is all that is needed for an act of theatre to be engaged.[1]

[1] Peter Brook, *The Empty Space*, Atheneum, New York, 1968, p 9.

Countless times in the course of a normal day, similar "acts of theatre" take place, with architecture as an ever-present backdrop playing its part in the drama.

How we understand these various languages of non-verbal communication has been the subject of the second part of this book. That we do understand each other at all, in our different modes of discourse, is testament to the presence of various shared underlying structures. With phenomenology, the problem centred on the notion of "intersubjectivity" and the extension of bodily experience beyond the individual's perceptual realm. Structuralism appeared to offer a social context for this experience, by embedding the individual in a network of pre-existing codes and conventions. At the same time, structuralist analysis failed to deal with historical change and the various brands of political criticism were shown to address this more specifically. In this conclusion we will consider further the whole question of historical tradition and the role of hermeneutic practices in the understanding of architecture. This is not to suggest that all these strategies could be incorporated in a single discipline, merely to show the relative merits of the different approaches to interpretation.

The critical element I have suggested in the title "critical hermeneutics" should serve to highlight a problem that will become apparent in the conventional understanding of the term. It is meant to suggest a certain vigilance towards the conservative tendencies of hermeneutics, and to restore the quality of questionableness with regard to historical traditions. As the French philosopher Jean-François Lyotard recommended, in *The Postmodern Explained*: "Everything that is received must be suspected, even if it is only a day old."[2]

The Hermeneutic Tradition

The dictionary definition of the word "hermeneutics" states that it concerns "interpretation, especially of scripture or literary texts". The

---

[2] Jean-François Lyotard, *The Postmodern Explained: Correspondence, 1982–1985*, translated by Don Barry *et al.*, University of Minnesota Press, Minneapolis, 1993, p 12.

reference to scripture immediately highlights the religious origins of the term, in both the Biblical and the ancient Greek practice of interpreting the "word of God". It derives from the Greek term used for the priest at the Delphic oracle, and also from Hermes, the wing-footed messenger-god. Hermes is the Greek equivalent of the angel in Christianity, the intermediary figure who communicates between people and the gods. We previously met this figure in the structuralist analysis of myth, as a device for explaining the causes of otherwise mysterious events. In hermeneutics, the god Hermes could be seen as a convenient metaphor, as a reminder of the idea that texts can be understood as "messages". The fact that texts require interpretation at all, as opposed to being merely carriers of neutral information, can also be inferred from the great disputes over interpretation that have marked the history of religions based on allegiance to a "founding document". The fragmentation of the Christian church within the last few hundred years is just one example of the scope for argument over the meaning of the "word of God". More dramatically, the seventh century split between Islam and Christianity, as well as the earlier Christian divergence from the Judaic Old Testament traditions, also shows how powerful the rewriting of texts can be when it is carried out under the name of ever more authentic interpretation.

The transformation of hermeneutics from a theological to an academic practice occurred with the eighteenth century expansion of scientific thinking in the humanities. As the contemporary French philosopher Paul Ricoeur described, in his essay "The Task of Hermeneutics", this could be seen as a shift from a regional to a general hermeneutics:

> Hermeneutics was born with the attempt to raise (Biblical) exegesis and (classical) philology to the level of a *Kunstlehre*, that is, a 'technology', which is not restricted to a mere collection of unconnected operations.[3]

---

[3] Paul Ricoeur, "The Task of Hermeneutics", in *Hermeneutics and the Human Sciences*, translated by John B. Thompson, Cambridge University Press, Cambridge, 1981, p 45.

Friedrich Schleiermacher is the figure most often credited with this innovation, a professor of theology who saw hermeneutics as a method for eliminating misunderstanding. His view that the understanding of a text depended on an understanding of the author can be seen as a consequence of Kant's notion of art as the product of individual genius. This Romantic concept of the individual as the origin of all meanings has been challenged, as we now know, by the twentieth century philosophies of structure. However, in the early nineteenth century rebellion against the constraints of classical traditions, a new impetus was added to the search for reliable principles of interpretation. Schleiermacher developed the notion of the "hermeneutic circle" to describe the interpretation of a text based on the relationship between part and whole. This could involve working from the details in order to build up a sense of the whole or, more reliably, working dialectically from both directions at once. Included in this process would be a study of the author's intentions which would again be compared with the actual content of the written text. The spatial figure of the circle also suggests another factor, the idea of a tradition being formed by a shared community of understanding. This again becomes important in later versions of hermeneutics where the idea of belonging becomes an influential theme.

This subjective approach was picked up by the next great innovator in hermeneutics, another German, Wilhelm Dilthey, who was a professor in Berlin from 1882. Dilthey opposed the philosophy of positivism that had followed the spread of science and instead tried to define the "human sciences" as dependent on a fundamentally different form of knowledge. He set out to do for the humanities what Kant had done for science, in the sense of inquiring into the "conditions of possibility of", not "pure" but *historical* reason. This was based on his distinction between explanation and understanding, where the former is the province of science and the latter of the humanities. Understanding for Dilthey was based on the historical context of the work, although the emphasis, as with Schleiermacher, was on the mental life of the author. It was only in the twentieth century with Martin Heidegger, in the book *Being and Time*, that the hermeneutic ques-

tion shifted dramatically once more. From being a question of epistemology concerning the different modes of knowledge, the issue then
became one of ontology, or the fundamental nature of human *being*.
In Heidegger's work, understanding became the basic mode of being,
and he set out to describe the world in which this being is situated. In
Chapter 3 we discussed the general direction of Heidegger's work as
he progressed from an emphasis on the everyday "lifeworld" towards
the gradual privileging of language. The discussion of tools provides a
good example of the understanding of objects according to context,
with the hermeneutic circle in this case consisting of a network of
related practices. An object thereby becomes meaningful in relation to
other pieces of equipment and, in Heidegger's terms this opens up a
world in which the object can be interpreted. There is also an antici-
patory dimension to this structure of contextual relations, in that it
necessarily precedes any particular object or act of perception. As
Heidegger writes in *Being and Time*, concerning this quality of pre-
existence:

> Whenever something is interpreted as something, the interpretation will
> be founded essentially upon fore-having, fore-sight, and fore-conception.
> An interpretation is never a presuppositionless apprehending of some-
> thing presented to us.[4]

The emphasis on language as the "house of being" that becomes a
characteristic of Heidegger's later writing is one of the themes picked
up by his student, a fellow German, Hans-Georg Gadamer. In his major
work, *Truth and Method*, published in German in 1960, he provided
an in-depth history of hermeneutics as well as developing his own contribution. Gadamer also picked up on Dilthey's notion of separating
explanation from understanding, claiming that the sciences' use of the
former relies on an alienation between object and observer. The ideal
of objectivity in the kind of knowledge sought by the sciences is seen
to be premised on a clear separation of interpreter from experiment.

[4] Martin Heidegger, *Being and Time*, translated by John Macquarrie and Edward
Robinson, Harper & Row, New York, 1962, pp 191–2.

The interpreter attempts to step outside the actual conditions of the experiment in order to achieve a level of neutrality and repeatability in their observations. Gadamer saw this condition of estrangement between observer and observed as the exact opposite of the experience of belonging that he felt was essential to hermeneutic understanding.

It is here that Gadamer's thought becomes prone to the charge of conservatism, because of his emphasis on the sense of belonging necessary to his concept of interpretation. In fact, a brief definition makes this point all too clear, when he claims that hermeneutics consists of: "the bridging of personal or historical distance between minds . . ."[5] This emphasis on the mind of the author recalls Schleiermacher's neo-Kantian notion, which held the genius or the individual to be the sovereign creator of original meanings. This notion is somewhat reinforced by Gadamer's description of understanding as dependent on the process of the "fusion of horizons". A person's horizon is the particular context in which the act of creation or interpretation takes place, being analogous to Heidegger's idea of the network of equipment that defines the tool. In a later essay, Gadamer emphasises this orientation towards the past when he illustrates his notion of art as a symbolic token of recollection:

> What does the word 'symbol' mean? Originally it was a technical term in Greek for a token of remembrance. The host presented his guest with the so-called *tessera hospitalis* by breaking some object in two. He kept one half for himself and gave the other half to his guest. If in thirty or fifty years time, a descendant of the guest should ever enter his house, the two pieces could be fitted together again to form a whole in an act of recognition.[6]

The "presence of the past" in Gadamer's concept of the experience of art as recollection is also suggested in his support of Heidegger's

---

[5] Hans-Georg Gadamer, "Aesthetics and Hermeneutics", in *Philosophical Hermeneutics*, translated by David E. Linge, University of California Press, Berkeley, CA, 1976, p 95.

[6] Hans-Georg Gadamer, "The Relevance of the Beautiful", in *The Relevance of the Beautiful and other Essays*, Robert Bernasconi (ed.), Cambridge University Press, Cambridge, 1986, p 31.

notion of language as the "house of being". He develops the idea of language as the privileged vehicle of cultural tradition and focuses in particular on writing as the ultimate conduit of historical truths:

> Nothing is so purely the trace of the mind as writing, but nothing is so dependent on the understanding mind either. In deciphering and inter-preting it, a miracle takes place: the transformation of something alien and dead into total contemporaneity and familiarity. This is like nothing else that comes down to us from the past. . . . Buildings, tools, the con-tents of graves – are weatherbeaten by the storms of time that have swept over them, whereas a written tradition, once deciphered and read, is to such an extent pure mind that it speaks to us as if in the present.[7]

This closing of the historical distance between the interpreter and the author of the text is the point of weakness in Gadamer's theory accord-ing to the criticism of Paul Ricoeur. He points out the necessity of retaining a sense of "alienation" between ourselves and things, in order to avoid the trap of believing that we can ever fully "recover" the past.

Ricoeur goes on to point out, in the essay mentioned above, that it is the very "tension between proximity and distance, which is essen-tial to historical consciousness".[8] Ricoeur develops this tension in his own work by returning to a concept of Heidegger's, where he describes the work of art as "opening up" or "revealing" a world. For Ricoeur this is a world in front of the text, not the world of the author behind it, and he saw the beginnings of this understanding in the earl-ier thinking of Dilthey:

> He indicated the direction in which historicism could overcome itself, without invoking a triumphant coincidence with some sort of absolute knowledge. But in order to pursue this discovery it is necessary to

---

[7] Hans-Georg Gadamer, *Truth and Method*, translated by Joel Weinsheimer and Donald G. Marshall, Sheed & Ward, London, 1989, p 163.
[8] Paul Ricoeur, "The Task of Hermeneutics", in *Hermeneutics and the Human Sciences*, translated by John B. Thompson, Cambridge University Press, Cambridge, 1981, p 61.

renounce the link between the destiny of hermeneutics and the purely psychological notion of the transference into another mental life; the text must be unfolded, no longer towards the author, but towards its immanent sense and towards the world which it opens up and discloses.[9]

The "Conflict" of Interpretations

The historical context of Ricoeur's first encounter with the philosophical background of hermeneutics is important for an understanding of the whole direction of his later work. It was during his imprisonment by the Nazis in the course of World War 2, that he discovered the writings of philosophers such as Husserl and Heidegger and the tradition of German historical scholarship. In making sense of the fact that German politics was not the inevitable result of German tradition, he also concluded that history must be continually open to reinterpretation. From this fact he developed the general principle of the "multiple meanings" of language, which was a major contribution to the *Conflict of Interpretations* and a basic principle of hermeneutics. He was also critical of the idealist tendency in Husserl's work in phenomenology, which attempted to interpret a "true" reality which is immediately apparent to the perceiving consciousness. Instead he insisted on the inescapable nature of the ongoing "task" of hermeneutics, which must be based on the suspicion of all immediately apparent meanings. He supported this endeavour in the work of various philosophers, who in their own different ways have developed a "hermeneutics of suspicion". He included in this category some we have already mentioned: Nietzsche's critique of the "genealogy" of rationality; Marx's exposure of capitalist ideology; and Freud's unmasking of the influence of the unconscious as it interferes in the everyday life of the conscious mind.

---

[9] Paul Ricoeur, "The Task of Hermeneutics", in *Hermeneutics and the Human Sciences*, translated by John B. Thompson, Cambridge University Press, Cambridge, 1981, p 53.

The instability of meaning in Ricoeur's notion of conflict was a theme in the more recent work of the Italian philosopher, Gianni Vattimo. Vattimo, who was also a student of Gadamer's, developed his own version of the plurality that is characteristic of postmodernist thinking. Just as Heidegger and, later, Derrida had developed a critique of Western philosophy based on the misguided search for foundations as the ultimate ground for absolute knowledge, Vattimo likewise characterised the current state of postmodernism in philosophy as a period of "post-foundationalism" or, more memorably, "weak thought". This situation lends significance to a range of previously marginalised discourses, such as Derrida makes clear in his discussion of fields not normally considered within philosophy. In *The Truth in Painting* Derrida focuses on the relationship between the work of art and the "frame", which turns out to be constitutive for the definition of art itself. Vattimo likewise takes up this theme of the centrality of the apparently marginal, both in his discussion of architectural ornament and in developing the concept of nihilism. Vattimo borrows this term from Nietzsche, to denote the "de-centreing" of the experiencing subject which, as we have mentioned already, has been a defining characteristic of modern philosophy.

For Vattimo, as for Ricoeur, this alienation of the individual subject from their position as "creator of meanings" has given new impetus to the idea that hermeneutic experience is actually a fundamental "mode of being". In a sense, our very existence demands a constant project of interpretation, given that there is always some uncertainty in any act of communication – whether the "interference" that phenomenology describes between the body and the world; or the arbitrariness of the signifier/signified pair defined by structural linguistics; or the invisible filter of ideology between us and our social relations – each of the models we have discussed in this book sets out an approach to this situation. As Vattimo described the legacy that Heidegger has left for the role of philosophy within the contemporary "alienated" world:

> Hermeneutics is not a theory that opposes an authenticity of existence founded on the privilege of the human sciences, to the alienation of the

rationalised society; it is rather a theory that tries to grasp the meaning of the transformation (of the idea) of Being that has been produced as a consequence of the techno-scientific rationalisation of our world.[10]

It should only be necessary here to say a few words about a "deconstructive" hermeneutics as a critical strategy of interpretation by way of conclusion. That the backward-looking emphasis in hermeneutics can conceivably be transformed within a more future-oriented practice is suggested by Derrida's affirmative attitude towards the past and his desire to open up issues previously repressed by the "dominant" histories. This dynamic approach to tradition also has a parallel with psychoanalysis, in the Freudian technique of working through the traumatic events of past experience. By taking up and restating the archetypal figures from the history of thought – at the same time as making explicit the basic ambiguities underlying their origin – the critical practice that Derrida advocates could also become a prelude to Heidegger's "opening up":

> This moment of doubling commentary should no doubt have its place in a critical reading. To recognise and respect all its classical exigencies is not easy and requires all the instruments of traditional criticism. Without this recognition and this respect, critical production would risk developing in any direction at all and authorise itself to say almost anything. But this indispensable guardrail has always only *protected*, it has never *opened*, a reading.[11]

The taking up and challenging of traditions within architecture has been an important element in each of the themes in this book. It is hoped that as part of this ongoing process of critical assessment and reinterpretation – necessitated by the role of buildings as "cultural texts" – that enough will have been gained through the hermeneutic

---

[10] Gianni Vattimo, *Beyond Interpretation: The Meaning of Hermeneutics for Philosophy*, translated by David Webb, Polity Press, London, 1997, p 110.
[11] Jacques Derrida, *Of Grammatology*, translated by Gayatri Chakravorty Spivak, Johns Hopkins University Press, Baltimore, MD, 1976, p 158.

project if, as Heidegger reminds us, architecture has again become "worthy of questioning".[12]

Suggestions for further reading

Background

Terry Eagleton, "Phenomenology, Hermeneutics, Reception Theory", in *Literary Theory: An Introduction*, University of Minnesota Press, Minneapolis, 1983, pp 54-90.

Hans-Georg Gadamer, "Aesthetics and Hermeneutics", in *Philosophical Hermeneutics*, translated by David E. Linge, University of California Press, Berkeley, CA, 1976, pp 95-104.

Paul Hamilton, *Historicism*, Routledge, London, 1996.

Fredric Jameson, "On Interpretation", in *The Political Unconscious: Narrative as a Socially Symbolic Act*, Routledge, London, 1989, pp 17-102.

Jean-François Lyotard, *The Postmodern Condition: A Report on Knowledge*, translated by Geoff Bennington and Brian Massumi, University of Minnesota Press, Minneapolis, 1984.

Paul Ricoeur, "The Task of Hermeneutics", in *Hermeneutics and the Human Sciences*, translated by John B. Thompson, Cambridge University Press, Cambridge, 1981, pp 43-62.

Gianni Vattimo, *Beyond Interpretation: The Meaning of Hermeneutics for Philosophy*, translated by David Webb, Polity Press, London, 1997.

Foreground

Alan Colquhoun, "From Bricolage to Myth, or How to Put Humpty-Dumpty Together Again", in *Essays in Architectural Criticism: Modern Architecture and Historical Change*, MIT Press, Cambridge,

---

[12] Martin Heidegger, "Building, Dwelling, Thinking", in *Poetry, Language, Thought*, translated by Albert Hofstadter, Harper & Row, New York, 1971, p 160. Reprinted in Neil Leach (ed.), *Rethinking Architecture*, Routledge, London, 1997.

MA, 1981. Reprinted in, K. Michael Hays (ed.), *Architecture Theory Since 1968*, MIT Press, Cambridge, MA, 1998, pp 336-46.

Peter Eisenman, "The End of the Classical: The End of the Beginning, the End of the End", in *Perspecta*, 21, 1984. Reprinted in Kate Nesbitt (ed.), *Theorising a New Agenda for Architecture: An Anthology of Architectural Theory 1965-95*, Princeton Architectural Press, New York, 1996, pp 212-27.

Vittorio Gregotti, *Inside Architecture*, translated by Wong and Zaccheo, MIT Press, Cambridge, MA, 1996.

Robert Mugerauer, *Interpreting Environments: Tradition, Deconstruction, Hermeneutics*, University of Texas Press, Austin, TX, 1995.

Joseph Rykwert, "Meaning and Building", in *Zodiac* 6, 1957. Reprinted in *The Necessity of Artifice*, Academy Editions, London, 1982, pp 9-16.

Dalibor Vesely, "Architecture and the Conflict of Representation" in *AA Files*, No. 8, January 1985, pp 21-38.

Bibliography

Adorno, Theodor, "Functionalism Today", in Neil Leach, editor, *Rethinking Architecture*, Routledge, London, 1997, pp 6-19.

Adorno, Theodor and Horkheimer, Max, *Dialectic of Enlightenment*, John Cumming, translator, Verso, London, 1979.

Alexander, Christopher, *et al.*, *A Pattern Language: Towns, Buildings, Construction*, Oxford University Press, New York, 1977.

—— *The Production of Houses*, Oxford University Press, New York, 1985.

Aristotle, "The Poetics", in *The Complete Works of Aristotle*, Jonathan Barnes, editor, Princeton University Press, Princeton, 1984.

Bachelard, Gaston, *The Psychoanalysis of Fire*, Alan C. M. Ross, translator, Beacon Press, Boston, 1964.

—— *The Poetics of Space*, Maria Jolas, translator, Beacon Press, Boston, 1969.

Bacon, Francis, *Essays*, J. M. Dent, London, 1994.

—— *Novum Organum*, Open Court, Chicago, 1994.

Banham, Reyner, *Theory and Design in the First Machine Age*, Architectural Press, London, 1960.

—— *The New Brutalism: Ethic or Aesthetic?*, Architectural Press, London, 1966.

Barthes, Roland, *Elements of Semiology*, Annette Lavers and Colin Smith, translators, Hill and Wang, New York, 1968.

—— *Mythologies*, Annette Lavers, translator, Harper Collins, London, 1973.

—— *Image-Music-Text*, Stephen Heath, translator, Noonday Press, New York, 1988.

—— "Semiology and the Urban", in Neil Leach, editor, *Rethinking Architecture*, Routledge, London, 1997, pp 166-172.

Basalla, George, *The Evolution of Technology*, Cambridge University Press, Cambridge, 1988.

Baudrillard, Jean, *The Gulf War Did Not Take Place*, Paul Patton, translator, Power Institute, University of Sydney, 1995.

Beardsley, Monroe, *Aesthetics: From Classical Greece to the Present, A Short History*, Macmillan, New York, 1966.

Benjamin, Andrew, "Eisenman and the Housing of Tradition", in *Architectural Design*, 1-2/1989, reprinted in Neil Leach, editor, *Rethinking Architecture*, Routledge, London, 1997, pp 286-301.

Benjamin, Walter, "The Work of Art in the Age of Mechanical Reproduction", in *Illuminations: Essays and Reflections*, Harry Zohn, translator, Schocken Books, New York, 1968.

Bergson, Henri, *Matter and Memory*, N. M. Paul and W. S. Palmer, translators, Zone Books, New York, 1988.

van Berkel, Ben, "A Day in the Life: Mobius House by UN Studio/van Berkel & Bos", *Building Design*, Issue 1385, 1999, p 15.

Blonsky, Marshall, editor, *On Signs*, Johns Hopkins University Press, Baltimore, MD, 1985.

Broadbent, Geoffrey, "A Plain Man's Guide to the Theory of Signs in Architecture", in *Architectural Design*, No. 47, 7-8/1978, pp 474-82, reprinted in Kate Nesbitt, editor, *Theorising a New Agenda for Architecture: An Anthology of Architectural Theory 1965-95*, Princeton Architectural Press, New York, 1996, pp 124-140.

Brook, Peter, *The Empty Space*, Atheneum, New York, 1968.

Buchanan, Peter, "Nostalgic Utopia", *Architects Journal*, 4 September/1985, pp 60-69.

Buckminster Fuller, R., *Nine Chains to the Moon*, Southern Illinois University Press, Carbondale, 1938.

Buck-Morss, Susan, *The Dialectics of Seeing: Walter Benjamin and the Arcades Project*, MIT Press, Cambridge, MA, 1989.

Caputo, John D., *Deconstruction in a Nutshell: A Conversation with Jacques Derrida*, Fordham University Press, New York, 1997.

Cassirer, Ernst, *An Essay on Man: An Introduction to a Philosophy of Human Culture*, Yale University Press, New Haven, 1944.

—— *The Philosophy of the Enlightenment*, Princeton University Press, Princeton, 1951.

—— *The Philosophy of Symbolic Forms*, 3 volumes, Ralph Manheim, translator, Yale University Press, New Haven, 1955-7.

de Certeau, Michel, *The Practice of Everyday Life*, Steven Rendall, translator, University of California Press, Berkeley, CA, 1984.

Colquhoun, Alan, *Essays in Architectural Criticism: Modern Architecture and Historical Change*, MIT Press, Cambridge, MA, 1981.

Conrads, Ulrich, editor, *Programmes and Manifestoes on 20th Century Architecture*, Lund Humphries, London, 1970.

Cook, Peter, editor, *Archigram*, Studio Vista, London, 1972.

Copernicus, Nikolaus, *On the Revolutions of Heavenly Spheres*, Charles G. Wallis, translator, Prometheus Books, Essex, 1996.

Debord, Guy, *Society of the Spectacle*, Black and Red, Detroit, 1983.

Derrida, Jacques, *Of Grammatology*, Gayatri C. Spivak, translator, Johns Hopkins University Press, Baltimore, 1976.

—— *Positions*, Alan Bass, translator, University of Chicago Press, Chicago, 1981.

—— "Point de Folie – maintenant de l'architecture", Kate Linker, translator, in *AA Files*, No. 12/Summer 1986, reprinted in Neil Leach, editor, *Rethinking Architecture*, Routledge, London, 1997, pp 324–347.

—— *The Truth in Painting*, Geoff Bennington and Ian McLeod, translators, University of Chicago Press, Chicago, 1987.

Derrida, Jacques and Eisenman, Peter, *Chora L Works*, Jeffrey Kipnis and Thomas Leeser, editors, Monacelli Press, New York, 1986.

Descartes, René, *Discourse on Method and The Meditations*, F. E. Sutcliffe, translator, Penguin Books, London, 1968.

—— "The World" and "Treatise on Man", in *The Philosophical Writings of Descartes*, Volume 1, John Cottingham *et al.*, translators, Cambridge University Press, Cambridge, 1985.

Dewey, John, *Art as Experience*, Perigee Books, New York, 1980.

Dreyfus, Hubert L., *Being-in-the-World: A Commentary on Heidegger's Being and Time,* Division I, MIT Press, Cambridge, MA, 1991.

Eagleton, Terry, *Literary Theory: An Introduction*, University of Minnesota Press, Minneapolis, 1983.

Eisenman, Peter, "Post-Functionalism" in *Oppositions*, 6/Fall 1976, reprinted in K. Michael Hays, editor, *Architecture Theory Since 1968*, MIT Press, Cambridge, MA, 1998, pp 236-9.

—— "The End of the Classical: The End of the Beginning, the End of the End", in *Perspecta*, 21, 1984, reprinted in Kate Nesbitt, editor, *Theorising a New Agenda for Architecture: An Anthology of Architectural Theory 1965-95*, Princeton Architectural Press, New York, 1996, pp 212-27.

—— *House of Cards*, Oxford University Press, New York, 1987.

Eisenman, Peter, *et al.*, *Five Architects: Eisenman, Graves, Gwathmey, Hejduk, Meier*, Oxford University Press, New York, 1975.

Michel Foucault, *The History of Sexuality, Volume I: An Introduction*, Robert Hurley, translator, Vintage Books, New York, 1990.

—— *The Order of Things: An Archaeology of the Human Sciences*, Vintage Books, New York, 1994.

—— *Discipline and Punish: The Birth of the Prison*, Alan Sheridan, translator, Vintage Books, New York, 1995.

—— "Space, Knowledge and Power", interview with Paul Rabinow, reprinted in, Neil Leach, editor, *Rethinking Architecture*, Routledge, London, 1997, pp 367-79.

Frampton, Kenneth, "Prospects for a Critical Regionalism", in *Perspecta*, 20/1983, reprinted in Kate Nesbitt, editor, *Theorising a New Agenda for Architecture: An Anthology of Architectural Theory 1965-95*, Princeton Architectural Press, New York, 1996, pp 470-82.

——— "Intimations of Tactility: Excerpts from a Fragmentary Polemic", in Scott Marble *et al.*, editors, *Architecture and Body*, Rizzoli, New York, 1988, unpaginated.

——— "Rappel a l'Ordre: The Case for the Tectonic" in *Architectural Design*, 3-4/1990, reprinted in Kate Nesbitt, editor, *Theorising a New Agenda for Architecture: An Anthology of Architectural Theory 1965-95*, Princeton Architectural Press, New York, 1996, pp 518-28.

——— *Modern Architecture: a Critical History*, Thames and Hudson, London, 1992.

Frascari, Marco, *Monsters of Architecture: Anthropomorphism in Architectural Theory*, Rowman and Littlefield, Savage, MD, 1991.

——— "The Tell-the-Tale Detail", *VIA*, No. 7, 1984. Reprinted in Kate Nesbitt, editor, *Theorising a New Agenda for Architecture: An Anthology of Architectural Theory 1965-95*, Princeton Architectural Press, New York, 1996.

Gadamer, Hans-Georg, *Philosophical Hermeneutics*, David E. Linge, translator, University of California Press, Berkeley, CA, 1976.

——— *The Relevance of the Beautiful and Other Essays*, Robert Bernasconi, editor, Cambridge University Press, Cambridge, 1986.

——— *Truth and Method*, Joel Weinsheimer and Donald G. Marshall, translators, Sheed & Ward, London, 1989.

Gandelsonas, Mario, "Linguistics in Architecture", in *Casabella*, No. 374, 2/1973, reprinted in K. Michael Hays, editor, *Architecture Theory Since 1968*, MIT Press, Cambridge, MA, 1998, pp 114-22.

Gelernter, Mark, *Sources of Architectural Form: A Critical History of Western Design Theory*, Manchester University Press, Manchester, 1995.

Gramsci, Antonio, *Selections from the Prison Notebooks*, Hoare and Nowell-Smith, translators, Lawrence and Wishart, London, 1971.

Graves, Michael, "A Case for Figurative Architecture", in Wheeler, Arnell and Bickford, editors, *Michael Graves: Buildings and Projects 1966-81*, Rizzoli, New York, 1982, pp 11-13. Reprinted in Kate Nesbitt, editor, *Theorising a New Agenda for Architecture: An Anthology of Architectural Theory 1965-95*, Princeton Architectural Press, New York, 1996, pp 86-90.

Gregotti, Vittorio, *Inside Architecture*, Wong and Zaccheo, translators, MIT Press, Cambridge, MA, 1996.

Hamilton, Paul, *Historicism*, Routledge, London, 1996.

Hawkes, David, *Ideology*, Routledge, London, 1996.

Hays, K. Michael, "From Structure to Site to Text: Eisenman's Trajectory", in *Thinking the Present: Recent American Architecture*, Hays and Burns, editors, Princeton Architectural Press, New York, 1990, pp 61–71.

—— editor, *Architecture Theory Since 1968*, MIT Press, Cambridge, MA, 1998.

Hegel, Georg Wilhelm Friedrich, *The Philosophy of History*, J. Sibree, translator, Dover, New York, 1956.

—— *Phenomenology of Spirit*, A. V. Miller, translator, Oxford University Press, Oxford, 1977.

—— *Introductory Lectures on Aesthetics*, Bernard Bosanquet, translator, Penguin Books, London, 1993.

Heidegger, Martin, *Being and Time*, John Macquarrie and Edward Robinson, translators, Harper & Row, New York, 1962.

—— "Building, Dwelling, Thinking" in *Poetry, Language, Thought*, Albert Hofstadter, translator, Harper and Row, New York, 1971, reprinted in Neil Leach, editor, *Rethinking Architecture*, Routledge, London, 1997, pp 100–109.

—— "The Origin of the Work of Art", in *Poetry, Language, Thought*, Albert Hofstadter, translator, Harper and Row, New York, 1971.

—— "... Poetically Man Dwells ...", in *Poetry, Language, Thought*, Albert Hofstadter, translator, Harper & Row, New York, 1971, reprinted in Neil Leach, editor, *Rethinking Architecture*, Routledge, London, 1997.

Hertzberger, Herman, "Building Order" in *VIA*, No. 7, Philadelphia, 1984.

—— *Lessons for Students in Architecture*, Ina Rike, translator, Uitgeverij 010, Rotterdam, 1991.

Hertzberger, Herman, *et al.*, *Aldo van Eyck*, Stichting Wonen, Amsterdam, 1982.

Hofstadter, Albert and Kuhns, Richard, editors, *Philosophies of Art and Beauty: Selected Readings in Aesthetics From Plato to Heidegger*, University of Chicago Press, Chicago, 1964.

Holl, Steven, *Intertwining*, Princeton Architectural Press, New York, 1996.

Husserl, Edmund, *The Crisis of European Sciences and Transcendental Phenomenology*, David Carr, translator, Northwestern University Press, Evanston, Illinois, 1970.

Jameson, Fredric, "Architecture and the Critique of Ideology", in Joan Ockman, editor, *Architecture, Criticism, Ideology*, Princeton Architectural Press, New York, 1985, reprinted in, K. Michael Hays, editor, *Architecture Theory Since 1968*, MIT Press, Cambridge, MA, 1998, pp 442–61.

—— *The Political Unconscious: Narrative as a Socially Symbolic Act*, Routledge, London, 1989.

—— *Postmodernism, or, The Cultural Logic of Late-Capitalism*, Verso, London, 1991.

—— "Is Space Political", in Cynthia Davidson, editor, *Anyplace*, MIT Press, Cambridge, MA, reprinted in Neil Leach, editor, *Rethinking Architecture*, Routledge, London, 1997, p 259.

Jencks, Charles, *The Language of Post-Modern Architecture*, Academy Editions, London, 1978.

Jencks, Charles, and Baird, George, editors, *Meaning in Architecture*, George Braziller, New York, 1969.

Jencks, Charles and Kropf, Karl, editors, *Theories and Manifestoes of Contemporary Architecture*, Academy Editions, London, 1997.

Kant, Immanuel, *Critique of Judgement*, J. H. Bernard, translator, Hafner Press, New York, 1951.

Kearney, Richard, *Modern Movements in European Philosophy*, Manchester University Press, Manchester, 1986.

Kenny, Anthony, *Descartes: A Study of his Philosophy*, Thoemmes Press, Bristol, 1997.

Kockelmans, Joseph K., *Phenomenology: The Philosophy of Edmund Husserl and its Interpretation*, Anchor Books, New York, 1967.

Kroll, Lucien, "Architecture and Bureaucracy", in Byron Mikellides, editor, *Architecture for People: Explorations in a New Humane Environment*, Studio Vista, London, 1980, pp 162–3.

Kruft, Hanno-Walter, *A History of Architectural Theory: From Vitruvius to the Present,* Princeton Architectural Press, New York, 1994.

Kuhn, Thomas, *The Structure of Scientific Revolutions*, University of Chicago Press, Chicago, 1970.

Leach, Neil, editor, *Rethinking Architecture: A Reader in Cultural Theory*, Routledge, London, 1997.

Lechte, John, *Fifty Key Contemporary Thinkers: From Structuralism to Postmodernity*, Routledge, London, 1994.

Le Corbusier, *Towards a New Architecture*, Frederick Etchells, translator, Architectural Press, London, 1946.

Lefebvre, Henri, *The Production of Space*, D. Nicholson-Smith, translator, Blackwell, Oxford, 1991.

Levi-Strauss, Claude, *Structural Anthropology*, Basic Books, New York, 1963.

—— *The Elementary Structures of Kinship*, Rodney Needham and James H. Bell, translators, Beacon Press, Boston, 1971.

—— *Tristes Tropiques*, John and Doreen Weightman, translators, Penguin Books, New York, 1992.

Loos, Adolf, *Spoken Into the Void: Collected Essays 1897–1900*, Jane O. Newman and John H. Smith, translators, MIT Press, Cambridge, MA, 1982.

Lukács, Georg, *History and Class Consciousness: Studies in Marxist Dialectics*, Rodney Livingstone, translator, Merlin Press, London, 1971.

Lynch, Kevin, *The Image of the City*, MIT Press, Cambridge, MA, 1960.

Lyotard, Jean-François, *The Postmodern Condition: A Report on Knowledge*, Geoff Bennington and Brian Massumi, translators, University of Minnesota Press, Minneapolis, 1984.

—— *The Postmodern Explained: Correspondence, 1982-1985*, Don Barry *et al.*, translators, University of Minnesota Press, Minneapolis, 1993.

Marcuse, Herbert, *The Aesthetic Dimension: Toward a Critique of Marxist Aesthetics*, Beacon Press, Boston, 1978.

—— *Eros and Civilisation: A Philosophical Inquiry into Freud*, Routledge, London, 1987.

—— *One-Dimensional Man: Studies in the Ideology of Advanced Industrial Society*, Beacon Press, Boston, 1991.

Marx, Karl and Engels, Friedrick, *The Marx-Engels Reader*, Robert C. Tucker, editor, Norton, New York, 1978.

Karl Marx and Frederick Engels, *The Communist Manifesto*, Eric Hobsbawm, editor, Verso, London, 1998.

McDonough, William, "Design Ecology, Ethics and the Making of Things" and "Hannover Principles", in Kate Nesbitt, editor, *Theorising a New Agenda for Architecture: An Anthology of Architectural Theory 1965-95*, Princeton Architectural Press, New York, 1996, pp 400-10.

McLellan, David, *Karl Marx*, Penguin Books, New York, 1975.

McLeod, Mary, "Architecture and Politics in the Reagan Era: From Postmodernism to Deconstructivism", *Assemblage*, 8, February 1989, reprinted in, K. Michael Hays, editor, *Architecture Theory Since 1968*, MIT Press, Cambridge, MA, 1998, pp 696-7.

Merleau-Ponty, Maurice, *Phenomenology of Perception*, Colin Smith, translator, Routledge, London, 1962.

—— "Eye and Mind", in *The Primacy of Perception*, James M. Edie, editor, Northwestern University Press, Evanston, IL, 1964.

—— "The Intertwining - The Chiasm", in *The Visible and the Invisible*, Alphonso Lingis, translator, Northwestern University Press, Evanston, IL, 1968.

Mugerauer, Robert, *Interpreting Environments: Tradition, Deconstruction, Hermeneutics*, University of Texas Press, Austin, TX, 1995.

—— "Derrida and Beyond", in Kate Nesbitt, editor, *Theorising a New Agenda for Architecture: An Anthology of Architectural Theory 1965-95*, Princeton Architectural Press, New York, 1996.

Mumford, Lewis, *Technics and Civilisation*, Harcourt, Brace, Jovanovich, New York, 1963.

Nesbitt, Kate, editor, *Theorising a New Agenda for Architecture: An Anthology of Architectural Theory 1965-95*, Princeton Architectural Press, New York, 1996.

Nietzsche, Friedrich, *The Birth of Tragedy*, Shaun Whiteside, translator, Penguin Books, London, 1993.

—— *On the Genealogy of Morality*, Keith Ansell-Pearson, editor, Cambridge University Press, Cambridge, 1994.

Norberg-Schulz, Christian, *Meaning in Western Architecture*, Studio Vista, London, 1975.

—— *Genius Loci: Towards a Phenomenology of Architecture*, Rizzoli, New York, 1980.

—— *Architecture: Meaning and Place, Selected Essays,* Rizzoli, New York, 1988.

—— "The Phenomenon of Place", in Kate Nesbitt, editor, *Theorising a New Agenda for Architecture: An Anthology of Architectural Theory 1965-95*, Princeton Architectural Press, New York, 1996, pp 414-28.

Norris, Christopher, *Deconstruction: Theory and Practice*, Routledge, London, 1991.

Ockman, Joan, editor, *Architecture Culture 1943-1968: A Documentary Anthology*, Rizzoli, New York, 1993.

Pawley, Martin, "Technology Transfer", in *Architectural Review*, 9/1987, pp 31-9.

—— *Buckminster Fuller*, Trefoil Publications, London, 1990.

Perez-Gomez, Alberto, *Architecture and the Crisis of Modern Science*, MIT Press, Cambridge, MA, 1983.

—— "The Renovation of the Body", in *AA Files*, No. 13/Autumn 1986, pp 26-9.

Perrault, Claude, *Ordonnance for the Five Kinds of Columns After the Method of the Ancients*, Indra Kagis McEwan, translator, Getty Center Publications, Santa Monica, 1993.

Plato, *The Republic*, I. A. Richards, translator, Cambridge University Press, Cambridge, 1966.

—— *The Collected Dialogues*, Edith Hamilton and Huntington Cairns, editors, Bollingen, Princeton, 1989.

Plotinus, *Enneads*, Stephen MacKenna, translator, Penguin Books, London, 1991.

Postman, Neil, *Technopoly: The Surrender of Culture to Technology*, Vintage Books, New York, 1993.

Rajchman, John, *Constructions*, MIT Press, Cambridge, MA, 1998.

Ricoeur, Paul, *Hermeneutics and the Human Sciences*, John B. Thompson, translator, Cambridge University Press, Cambridge, 1981.

Rogers, Richard, *Architecture: A Modern View*, Thames and Hudson, London, 1990.

Rossi, Aldo, *The Architecture of the City*, Diane Ghirardo and Joan Ockman, translators, Oppositions Books, MIT Press, Cambridge, MA, 1982.

Rowe, Colin, and Koetter, Fred, *Collage City*, MIT Press, 1978.

Rykwert, Joseph, "Meaning and Building", in *Zodiac* 6, 1957, reprinted in *The Necessity of Artifice*, Academy Editions, London, 1982, pp 9–16.

—— *The Dancing Column : On Order in Architecture*, MIT Press, Cambridge, MA, 1996.

de Saussure, Ferdinand, *Course in General Linguistics*, Wade Baskin, translator, McGraw-Hill, New York, 1966.

Singer, Peter, *Hegel*, Oxford University Press, Oxford, 1983.

Smithson, Alison, editor, *Team 10 Primer*, MIT Press, Cambridge, MA, 1968.

Smithson, Alison and Peter, *Without Rhetoric: An Architectural Aesthetic 1955–72*, Latimer New Dimensions, London, 1973.

Snow, C. P., *The Two Cultures and the Scientific Revolution*, Cambridge University Press, Cambridge, 1961.

de Sola-Morales, Ignasi, *Differences: Topographies of Contemporary Architecture*, Graham Thompson, translator, MIT Press, Cambridge, MA, 1997.

Steiner, George, *Martin Heidegger*, University of Chicago Press, Chicago, 1991.

Tafuri, Manfredo, "Toward a Critique of Architectural Ideology", *Contropiano* I, January–April 1969, reprinted in K. Michael Hays, editor, *Architecture Theory Since 1968*, MIT Press, Cambridge, MA, 1998.

—— *Architecture and Utopia: Design and Capitalist Development*, Barbara Luigia La Penta, translator, MIT Press, Cambridge, MA, 1976.

Tschumi, Bernard, *Architecture and Disjunction*, MIT Press, Cambridge, MA, 1994.

Turner, John F. C., *Housing By People*, Marion Boyars, London, 1976.

Utzon, Jorn, "Platforms and Plateaus", in *Zodiac*, No. 10, Milan, 1962.

Vattimo, Gianni, *Beyond Interpretation: The Meaning of Hermeneutics for Philosophy*, David Webb, translator, Polity Press, London, 1997.

Venturi, Robert, *Complexity and Contradiction in Architecture*, Architectural Press, London, 1977.

Venturi, Robert *et al.*, *Learning From Las Vegas*, MIT Press, Cambridge, MA, 1997.

Vesalius, Andreas, *The Illustrations from the Works of Andreas Vesalius of Brussels*, Dover Publications, New York, 1973.

Vesely, Dalibor, "Architecture and the Conflict of Representation", in *AA Files*, No. 8, January 1985, pp 21–38.

Vico, Giambattista, *The New Science of Giambattista Vico*, Thomas G. Bergin and Max H. Fisch, translators, Cornell University Press, Ithaca, 1984.

Viollet-le-Duc, E. E., *Lectures on Architecture*, 2 volumes, Benjamin Bucknall, translator, Dover, New York, 1987.

—— *The Foundations of Architecture*, Barry Bergdoll & Kenneth D. Whitehead, translators, George Braziller, New York, 1990.

Vitruvius, *On Architecture*, Frank Granger, translator, Harvard University Press, Cambridge, MA, 1983.

Weber, Max, *The Protestant Ethic and the Spirit of Capitalism*, Talcott Parsons, translator, Routledge, London, 1992.

Wigley, Mark, *The Architecture of Deconstruction: Derrida's Haunt*, MIT Press, Cambridge, MA, 1993.

Wittkower, Rudolf, *Architectural Principles in the Age of Humanism*, Academy Editions, London, 1998.

Wotton, Henry, *The Elements of Architecture*, Charlottesville, VA, 1968.

Wright, Frank Lloyd, *Writings and Buildings*, Edgar Kaufmann and Ben Raeburn, editors, New American Library, New York, 1974.

Zumthor, Peter, *Thinking Architecture*, Maureen Oberli-Turner, translator, Lars Muller Publishers, Baden, 1998.

Index